SANDY SANDERSON

INTAKE
131

Nineteen weeks as a
Rhodesian Army Officer Cadet

SANDY SANDERSON

INTAKE
131

Nineteen weeks as a
Rhodesian Army Officer Cadet

MEREO
CIRENCESTER

Mereo Books

1A The Wool Market Dyer Street Cirencester Gloucestershire GL7 2PR
An imprint of Memoirs Publishing www.mereobooks.com

Intake 131: 978-1-86151-334-2

First published in Great Britain in 2015
by Mereo Books, an imprint of Memoirs Publishing

The address for Memoirs Publishing Group Limited can be found at
www.memoirspublishing.com

The Memoirs Publishing Group Ltd Reg. No. 7834348

The Memoirs Publishing Group supports both The Forest Stewardship Council® (FSC®) and
the PEFC® leading international forest-certification organisations. Our books carrying both the
FSC label and the PEFC® and are printed on FSC®-certified paper. FSC® is the only
forest-certification scheme supported by the leading environmental organisations including
Greenpeace. Our paper procurement policy can be found at
www.memoirspublishing.com/environment

Typeset in 11/18pt Bembo
by Wiltshire Associates Publisher Services Ltd. Printed and bound in Great Britain by
Printondemand-Worldwide, Peterborough PE2 6XD

Dedicated to the boys and old boys of Prince Edward School
who lost their lives during the Rhodesian War.

Preface

This recollection of nineteen weeks spent at School of Infantry, Gwelo, Rhodesia, from April to August 1973 has come about as a result of my keeping a diary, for the first and only time in my life, and managing to add a substantial entry each and every day. Without that, this account would not have materialised.

These nineteen weeks constituted the training part of my National Service. National Service had been four and a half months until early 1965, then nine months until late 1972 and then, starting in January 1973, just short of a year.

I don't really know what prompted me to take the trouble to write the diary. Perhaps, essentially, I wanted a fairly comprehensive record of what was to happen during training. I used ten Croxley Pen Carbon Books.

There are no heroic acts in this account. Several of our officers and instructors were heroes with gallantry medals to prove it but for us, the national service Officer Cadets, it was a case of "mudding through" as best we could. Our civilian mentality must have been very trying for those training us.

I have strived to present an accurate record of what happened with no embellishments and nothing apocryphal. I hope I have succeeded. In the body of the manuscript and index, ranks of Rhodesian Army personnel are given as they were in 1973 or 1967.

Reading through my diary, it seems to me that we covered much during those four and a half months and that the training was very thorough, with a strong emphasis on the academic as well as the practical. I have made a point of describing in detail what we were taught, what we were trained in and how this training took place.

In this account I give the composition of the Rhodesian Army in 1973. I realise that this is not completely comprehensive but it does give a good general idea. I also elaborate on the nature of tactics taught to us in 1973 at Platoon Commander level. Most of this can be found with a careful search on the internet: try looking up "section battle drills" or "Drake shoots" – so there are no "trade secrets" given away!

I also include comment, in some cases, on what happened after the 1973 events recorded in my original diary.

The Rhodesian War came about as a result of Rhodesia's Unilateral Declaration of Independence on 11 November 1965, thus maintaining a white majority government and denying unimpeded progress towards universal franchise. African nationalists decided that only "through the barrel of a gun" would they achieve this and decided to train outside the country, arm, courtesy of the Eastern European states, and infiltrate.

In 1973 the Rhodesian War (1965-1979) was restricted to the north east of the country (called the Hurricane Operational area) with an escalation initiated by attacks on farms near Mount Darwin in December 1972. The escalation intensified with the withdrawal of Portuguese armed forces from Mozambique in 1974 and 1975 when the country was given its independence, hence freeing up a huge slice of the Rhodesian border for infiltration. This resulted in other operational areas being opened up as time went on.

Necessarily, I suppose, things are described as I saw them and although I have tried to put the others person's point of view across, even this is as I remember it. I have included a few memories, not of my own but of others. In this regard I would like to acknowledge help from Digby Neuhoff, Charlie Lenegan and Pete Addison, who were with me on my course and are mentioned often. I would also like to acknowledge the considerable help I have been given by WO2 Reg Ayling, Lieutenant Colonel Jerry Strong MLM BCR and Brigadier Vic Walker SM & Bar MMM JCD with regards to Rhodesian Army personnel and establishment. Brigadier Walker was a Major in 1973 and is also mentioned in my book.

Our experience was tougher than some and not as tough as others but followed the general format of the basic training that all men in the armed forces went through.

Part and parcel of the whole thing were the choice phrases, varied, colourful and more often than not profane, which were regularly used by our trainers. Any Rhodesian drill instructor could string a sentence together consisting entirely of expletives, apart from the odd indefinite article, and make perfect sense.

Being an Officer Cadet made no difference to our treatment in this regard. Certainly we were never called "sir", as is the case for Officer Cadets in the British Army.

Over the years friends and family, in particular my wife, Patsy, have suggested that I publish the diary in the form of a short book. They felt it would provide a detailed account of basic training as it was in the early seventies in the Rhodesian Army and that people would find it interesting, especially those who had been through it. Whatever unit we were in, all of us experienced basic training. It would certainly evoke many memories of things half-forgotten.

All this happened over 40 years ago, quite a long passage of time, and men from our course are now into their sixties. Certainly anyone involved in the war in Rhodesia as a member of the services would now have to be at least in their fifties. Perhaps publication is not before time.

I.M. Sanderson | **March 2015**

Wednesday 11 April 1973

I had finished two days' leave from my job as an Internal Affairs Cadet in Kariba pending a year's National Service and had come from the Jameson House staff pub at Prince Edward School. This is the school where I had taught until the end of 1972 before taking the job with Internal Affairs.

Piet de Bruijn, a teacher of Afrikaans at Prince Edward, had kindly given me a lift to the Salisbury station to catch the troop train to Bulawayo. It had been an excellent evening so far; a couple of beers and a couple of laughs in good company. Now the tough times were to begin.

Most young men about to start National Service, if they were honest, felt a certain amount of apprehension. There were the stories from the "old sweats" about extremely dangerous Sergeant-Majors, shine parades and hours of drill on the bitumen square with, from all accounts, very little sleep.

For me, these stories were supplemented by real-life experience, six weeks spent at the School of Infantry, Gwelo, on the 1967 Regular Officer's Course. Nightmarish memories surfaced of the dreaded Sergeant Basil Lentner, Sergeant Herman Nortje, WO2 Harry Springer and WO1 Peter Cooper as I walked through the station entrance. If anything, the stories I had heard vastly underplayed the experience which I and the other poor unfortunates of Intake 131 were about to endure.

1

At the station entrance I bumped into Gerald Fitzgerald, the 1972 Head Boy of Prince Edward, and got chatting.

"I didn't know you had been called up", said Gerald. "You know that Kevin Ravenhill and Nigel Willis have also been called up?"

We talked for a while, then, wishing me all the best, he left and I mused on the fact that Kevin and Nigel had been at Prince Edward the previous year in Form 4. I found out later that Phil Pryke, also a Prince Edward old boy, School Prefect and very good sportsman, was in our intake.

I walked down the platform, stepped onto the train, found a place in the first compartment I came to, put my suitcase on the rack and looked to see if there was anybody else I knew on the platform. By coincidence, along the platform came Kevin Ravenhill and Nigel Willis, who had bumped into each other earlier and stayed together, perhaps for moral support. To my surprise they saw me, did a double take and then came into my compartment.

Normally, boys of that era would make tracks in the opposite direction on spotting a teacher, but this situation was incongruous and their curiosity was too much of a factor to stop them interrogating their former schoolmaster. They simply could not believe that "Rusty" had been called up!

The incongruity was not lost on me either. My father, a veteran of the First and Second World Wars, once talked of being in the trenches with his old Latin teacher – an amusing story, only half believed. Well, as they say, truth is stranger than fiction.

Most of us on the train had no one to see us off, but some were saying goodbye to girlfriends and a very limited number to wives and there were a few emotional moments. Most of us by the end of the war would experience leaving loved ones for weeks at a time over and over again as it dragged on. Sadly many relationships did not survive the war.

The train was "dry" – no bar or dining car. Just as well really, as arriving at Llewellin Barracks with too much of a hangover could be hazardous. We engaged in nervous conversation for a while, then settled down to sleep as best we could with the next day's anticipated ordeal playing on our minds. It didn't take a brain surgeon to work out that we could be in for a bit of a torrid time.

Thursday 12 April

We awoke with the sun. Looking outside, we could see the train snaking along the tracks with the flats on either side. The Matabeleland grassland with its stunted acacias stretched to the horizon.

After about an hour the train pulled up at Heany Junction about 20km ENE of Bulawayo. Frenzied shouts from a group of Corporals greeted us.

"Double up you gungy bastards, get off the train! Get on the RLs!"

We surmised that "RLs" were the Army trucks that were standing by. We climbed onto the trucks as quickly as we could and they drove off, taking the dirt back-roads to Llewellin Barracks, a distance of about 2 km.

When we arrived the shouting started again.

"Line up in three ranks on the road!"

A very limited number of the recruits had had military experience, school cadet or otherwise, so even this simple manoeuvre took time with the NCOs pushing and shoving bodies into place.

"You will now transfer your bags to your weakest hand."

This was a bit of bad luck for me. I had a large suitcase with, among other things, an iron to help me in the "boning" of boots, a tip I had picked up from my experience with the Regular Officer's Course.

We were then marched about 300 metres to Lecture Room 4, came to a ragged halt and turned left to face the building.

"First rank, right turn! I said first rank, you fucking morons!"

Some of the aspiring soldiers in the second and third ranks had also turned right.

"Now line up in front of the lecture room."

It took some minutes before all 200 recruits had deposited their kit in Lecture Room 4. Company Sergeant Major Longuet-Higgins (B Company), who had been watching proceedings, took command.

"All right then, let's see how you drill. B Company, company

4

attention! Company will move to the right in threes, right turn. By the centre, quick march."

We were a motley crew, a polyglot bunch, moving with Brownian motion, as Pete Addison was to later recall, and we shuffled off as best we could to the dining hall, were fallen out, lined up in single file rank by rank and led in to our first Army breakfast off tin plates. The food was excellent. One thing about the Rhodesian Army was that the troops were always fed well, with good nourishing meals. The old adage about an army marching on its stomach was taken seriously. Witness the fact that the new arrivals were fed as a first priority.

Next stop was a large hangar housing a basketball court and squash courts for a medical inspection, haircuts, if deemed necessary, and attestation. These proceedings took about two hours and the recruits were then officially under Army discipline.

A rumour went around that one of the group had been picked up that morning at Bulawayo Airport trying to leave the country on a flight to South Africa to avoid the "call up". We never did find out if he existed or, if so, who he was.

On to another building to be issued with knife, fork, spoon, mug, 2 sheets, pillow, pillowcase, mosquito net and canvas mattress cover. Then on to the barrack rooms to drop the kit off on the beds, each with a blanket and a mattress already there, and then off straight away to another hangar to be told to strip down to underpants to be issued with, in army parlance, 1 cap camouflage, 1 beret green, 1 badge beret, 1 flash beret, 2 shirts green, 2 shirts camouflage, 1 jersey green, 3 vests green, 1 jacket camouflage, 3 pairs denims camouflage, 2 pairs shorts KG, 1 pair shorts PT, 1 belt stick, 1 belt stable, 3 pairs underpants green, 4 pairs socks grey, 1pair leggings, 1 pair hose-tops khaki, 1 pair boots stick, 1 pair boots combat, 1 pair boots hockey, 1 brush clothes, 1 brush boot, 1 brush hair, 1 brush shaving, 1 brush tooth and 1 razor (no blades).

We were told to get dressed in a camouflage cap, camouflage jacket, PT shorts, grey socks and hockey boots (to make us look as ridiculous as possible). We stuffed the rest of the gear and our "civvies" into a white canvas kit bag. We were then marched back to the barrack rooms.

In the barrack rooms we were told to get into denim order, namely camouflage cap (later on it would be beret with Rhodesia Regiment badge and flash), camouflage shirt and longs, stick belt, grey socks, leggings and combat boots. We were then marched at the double (running) to lunch to experience for the first time the army principle of "hurry up and wait". With limited seating, about 80 at a time, the wait outside for the last platoon in (64 in a platoon to fit in with intake numbers) was up to an hour.

Next, off to the cinema hall, where we sat down and were given a lecture by the Commanding Officer (CO), Depot Rhodesian Regiment (DRR), Lt Colonel Thompson. He welcomed the intake to Llewellin Barracks but wasted no time in stating a long list of rules, with particular reference as to what not to do and the consequences of any offence. He saved his *pièce de résistance* for last.

"If you are found in possession of drugs you will be given four to eight weeks DB at Brady Barracks. You will not find this a pleasant experience. Although the MPs at Brady are very fair, they are also very hard. Carry on Sergeant Major."

Sergeant Major Longuet-Higgins called us to attention and saluted Lieutenant Colonel Thompson as he walked out.

The reference to DB (Detention Barracks) as opposed to CB (Confined to Barracks) was taken very seriously by most. We had all heard stories, sometimes first hand, of what happened to people in the infamous Detention Barracks at Brady in Bulawayo. MPs (Military Police) would "rev" the hell out of all inmates, physically and mentally, from dawn to dusk. Inspections were very severe. Woe betide anyone with the least thing wrong with his cell or appearance. People came out of DB very thin, very fit and very smart! The time spent there was added to the period of military service.

While we were musing over the Lieutenant Colonel's observations Sergeant Major Longuet-Higgins explained that they would be choosing a small number of people, after a two-day selection process, for officer training at the School of Infantry, Gwelo. This officer training course would take place at the same time as the rest of the intake was training at Llewellin Barracks.

He then called for volunteers. There were 70 takers. I was one of them.

We volunteers were marched to the hospital for another medical examination, a little more stringent than the morning one, and then back to barracks to change into PT kit and camouflage jacket for supper.

After supper some of the volunteers in my barrack room, including myself, realised that we still had not collected our "civvy" kit from Lecture Room 4. We decided to leave the barrack room and double in a squad to collect our kit. It had been made very clear that any movement about the camp was to be at the double! Things went according to plan apart from a nasty moment when a rabid Regimental Sergeant Major Butler screamed at us, "Get a grip of that bloody squad!" He didn't appear to care much for recruits.

The rest of the evening was spent furiously "jacking up" kit, particularly stick belt and leggings, which had to be polished black. Company roll call was at 7.15pm (1915hrs), outside on the tarmac, with lights out at 10.00pm (2200hrs).

Friday 13 April

Breakfast was at 0545hrs in denim order, no inspections as yet with settling in routine until Monday. After breakfast, volunteers for OSB, colloquially known as and pronounced as "osbies" (standing for Officer Selection Board), were marched to a small dining room and, sitting really cramped up opposite and next to each other, wrote Intelligence and Aptitude Tests.

Next on the agenda was an appreciation. We volunteers were given an imaginary problem situation and told to write out a viable solution to the problem. We then divided up into three groups of about 23 each in three separate rooms and sat in a half circle, with a couple of examining officers observing, to discuss the problem.

This was the first opportunity for the examining staff, all officers, to watch and "sum up" the candidates. I spoke first and gave my solution. Someone else then spoke, but in a very short time there was a cacophony of voices with everyone trying to get their point across. I was quite glad that I had spoken first. The officers had to intervene to settle things down and the discussion continued until the officers terminated it.

Over the years, many OSB candidates experienced the selection process and took part in the discussion over the appreciation. Tidge Cartwright and Pete Stewart, teaching colleagues of mine, when they were on OSB with different intakes, each appointed themselves as chairman for the discussion and kept control of it. Needless to say both were selected for officer training and both were commissioned at the end.

We aspiring officers were then taken back to the dining room to write an essay. We were given the three topics of "Co-education", "The Most Embarrassing Day of My Life" and "A Great Soldier".

A self-appointed squad "smart arse" asked the NCO who had read out the titles "Must it be fact or fiction?" We weren't sure if he understood the question, as at first he seemed flummoxed, but his reply when it came was terse and to the point. "It doesn't fucking matter!"

On the principle that officers are not supposed to be embarrassed or know much about education, I chose "A Great Soldier" and wrote about Claude Auchinleck.

After lunch we were divided up into smaller groups to give three-minute talks on any chosen subject. I had been doing a sub-aqua diving course in Kariba and decided to do a talk on this. Regrettably, Tollie Wade, destined to be selected for Gwelo, chose diving as his topic, just before I was about to speak, so I had to extemporise. I quickly chose sky-diving as my topic and put together a relatively unplanned talk at very short notice.

After the talk Sergeant Major Longuet-Higgins spoke to us. He explained that only a limited number would be selected for Gwelo but that those who were not selected would still have an opportunity to join the LTU (Leadership Training Unit) at Llewellin later on. He then read out the names of those who would go through to the second day of the selection process. There were 27 left out of 70. I was one of the 27.

We doubled back to the barracks, changed into PT kit and went to supper. We then continued to work on our kit. The rest of the intake had been polishing and cleaning all day and so there was quite a bit of catching up to do.

Nigel Willis came up to me in the barrack room. "What was osbies like, sir?" he blurted out.

"For God's sake don't call me sir." I said, "I'm just a recruit like you."

"Sorry sir", replied Nigel."

Indeed, old habits die hard.

Later Nigel Willis became a regular and passed the selection for and joined the SAS. Sadly he was killed in action, on 14 February 1974.

After company roll call some of the senior intake (129) came into the barrack room, seemingly on their way back from the canteen. They called the recruits to attention by their beds. Most of the new intake stood immediately to attention, but a couple of the older ones had heard how some "veterans" would try it on with the newcomers and took them on, asking for their rank. The senior intake backed off immediately, knowing that they had been specifically ordered by their instructors not to interfere with the new intake and fearing the consequences. They mumbled something about "just visiting" and left.

I managed to scribble a page on the day's events in a Croxley carbon pad in the last ten minutes before lights out. I had determined to write a sort of diary of "Army life" but was finding time scarce.

Saturday 14 April

Breakfast was again at 0545hrs. We, the 27 "osbie survivors", doubled to the training area, filled in a form for personal details and were divided into three groups to tackle the obstacle course. We were kept under the closest scrutiny while we took turns to lead our group across nine different imaginary obstacles. We were given bibs with numbers on them and told to refer to each other by number only.

Sergeants briefed the groups on each obstacle.

"Here we have a swollen river with two stumps sticking out of the water. Your task is to get yourselves and a 44-gallon drum to the other side without falling in the river using only the two poles you see before you. Number fifteen, you are in charge!"

I was number fifteen and looked at the obstacle. It was the same one that my group had eventually negotiated when I had been on the Regular Officers OSB in December 1966 and, luckily, I remembered how we had negotiated it. I was able, very efficiently, to get the whole group plus drum across. Certainly this seemed to be a stroke of luck, although we suspected that more important than success in crossing the obstacle was how one handled men.

The process took until lunch, with the candidates experiencing varied degrees of success. Nine more recruits were eliminated and the remaining 18 brought back for interviews with a panel of six regular officers in the afternoon.

The final group was mustered outside the interview room and told, when the time came to enter the room, to march in smartly, halt as best they could, salute as best they could and then await orders.

I was about fifth in the group to go in. I marched in and saluted.

"Sit down", said one of the Officers, indicating a chair. In retrospect I realize that this officer was Major Walker, President of the National Service OSB. I sat down with officers to the front and left and right. Pertinent questions were then fired at me. "Why do you want to be an officer"? "How do you think you will handle men"?

After about ten minutes I marched out, wondering how I had coped with the barrage.

At the end of the interviewing process the moment of truth came. The recruits were lined up and the names of those to go to Gwelo were announced in alphabetical order. Sergeant Major Longuet-Higgins did the honours.

"Those selected are Addison, Barlow, Birch, Evans, Green, Lenegan, Lindsay, Mutch, Neuhoff, Nupen, Richardson, Sanderson and Wade". I was in. Thirteen out of 200 in the intake were off to School of Infantry, to leave on Monday.

It was then back to the barrack room, where we spent what was left of the afternoon and evening polishing stick boots. The trick here was to iron them, taking care to stay away from the stitching, to get them hot and smooth and then to liberally apply black Kiwi polish and rub it in with a cloth. It was a long and arduous process.

There was a long line of people wanting to borrow the iron. Somebody left it on too long and the element blew. Fortunately for me, my boots were almost ready by the time this happened.

At about 9.00pm (2100hrs) a few blokes from the other intakes came into the barracks, among them my old mate Alan Anderson whom I had taught with at Prince Edward. Also with him were some Prince Edward Old Boys: Mark McNulty, of future golf fame, Johnnie Whitfield, tragically killed in the war in 1978, Tony Rigby, Keith Webster, "DG" Harris and Maxie MacCallum.

Alan Anderson tried to persuade me, and others, to go with them to the canteen for a quick beer. 131 had been very clearly and very specifically ordered not to go anywhere near the canteen. I politely refused the offer. Apart from the fact that I had work to do, being caught there would not have done much for my chances of getting to Gwelo. Nobody from 131 went to the canteen in the end.

Sunday 15 April

The traditional day of rest was spent by the intake polishing and cleaning in anticipation of the first inspection to be held on Monday. Most worked on their stick-belt brasses. The method was to spend several hours sandpapering them, then several more working on them with the finer emery paper before finishing them off, to get rid of the minor scratches, with ceiling board.

The barrack rooms for 131 were new and well-appointed brick buildings, much to the chagrin of 130 (A Company) and 129 (C Company), who had slightly inferior accommodation in the old barrack rooms. There were 32 beds in each barrack room, 16 on each side, with lockers next to each bed and four large sets of lockers down the middle. The floors were concrete, one door at each end and ten windows on each side. It was to be home for the next 19 weeks for most of us.

During the morning we worked on "jacking up" our kit.

The intake were also handed a sheet with the names of important personnel for B Company on it.

DRR LLEWELLIN BARRACKS

Lt Colonel Thompson	CO
Major Walker	2 IC
Captain Cameron-Davies	Adjutant
WO1 Butler	RSM

B COMPANY

Major Morris	OC
Captain Puren	2 IC
Captain du Preez,	Training Officer
WO2 Longuet-Higgins	CSM
Sgt Kluckow	CQMS
No 4 Platoon Commander	Sgt Platt
No 5 Platoon Commander	Cpl De Wet
No 6 Platoon Commander	C/Sgt Botha

Platoons are supposed to be commanded by an officer, but there was a serious shortage of commissioned ranks, hence the national service O.S.B. but Sergeant Platt, Corporal De Wet and Colour Sergeant Botha were experienced regulars and probably knew their job better than any recently commissioned men.

Their corporals were rear rank instructors, national servicemen who had been on a crash drill and basic instruction course. Considering their limited experience and time spent in the Army, they did a really good job and allowed regular Army junior NCOs to be deployed at the "sharp end".

When the first national servicemen were commissioned in 1966, the regular NCOs were reluctant to accept them with only four and a half months' training, as opposed to a year for the regulars. As time went by, however, the regulars learnt to take each national serviceman as they found him. There were, over the years, some excellent soldiers among them.

The day went by all too quickly with interruptions for meals and the evening roll call. With 200 names to read out, this always took time, especially if the duty NCOs decided to give the odd quiet "rev". Such was the case this time round.

"Shut up in the rear ranks, you bloody fuck pigs!" bawled the Corporal.

Silence reigned.

"Addison!"

Addison, coming to attention, replied as loudly as he could. "Corporal!"

The roll call went on. "Groen!" No answer! "GROEN!"

The Corporal was becoming irritated. A belated reply came from the ranks. "Corporal!"

It was too late. The Corporal was apoplectic. "Why didn't you answer your name the first time, you fucking spunk bubble? Come here!"

The unfortunate Groen spent the rest of the roll call trying to climb a nearby telephone pole with a brick in each hand, to the none-too-refined exhortations of two other corporals. He did not have much success.

Lights out came, as usual, before the men in the barrack room were ready.

Monday 16 April

The barrack room woke early, at about 0430hrs, to have the proverbial shit, shower and shave in old washrooms under a single dull light bulb. Two vital things were missing, toilet paper and plugs in the sinks. However hot water was readily available.

Then, for the "Gwelo thirteen", the last breakfast at Llewellin, in denim order. Two hundred lined up in three ranks. I had been extremely lucky, always in the first rank to go in, no waiting.

After wishing the rest of the intake all the best, we selectees went to hand in the kit first issued to us and then carried the rest, civvy and military, to the B Company HQ for the trip to

Gwelo. We climbed onto the RL and were off with Sergeant Major Longuet-Higgins' final words of advice echoing in our ears: "It's all very smart at School of Infantry. If it moves salute it, if it doesn't move whitewash it. Good luck to you all."

Having had no visits to the canteen at Llewellin, a stop at a garage on the way, to buy cokes and crisps, was a welcome break. On the road again with overtaking motorists giving us cheery waves, we must at least have looked like "troopies".

We finally arrived at Gwelo. I looked out from the RL as we entered the gates through the boom. As far as I could see, the place had not changed since 1967. The rugby field, the drill-square and regimental wing all looked exactly the same. There were in fact a few new buildings, barrack rooms and lecture rooms, but that was about all.

We were met by Colour Sergeant Wales of the SAS. This looked like a good omen and as it turned out he was a most conscientious instructor. He fell us in, introduced himself and then doubled us to our new home, Slim West barracks, named after Field Marshall William Slim of Second World War fame. We noticed that blankets and linen were on the beds. Next to us was an empty barrack room, Slim East. We off-loaded and stored our gear as instructed and were then doubled to the National Service Officer Cadets' Mess for lunch.

There Colour Wales left us in the hands of the PMC (President of the Mess Committee) with instructions to be outside Taungup at 1400hrs. The PMC from the senior intake (129) gave us a talk on mess etiquette.

Berets and belts were to be left on pegs outside the mess. As junior intake we were allowed in the national serviceman cadets' bar but the consumption of alcohol was forbidden until the end of first phase, in six weeks' time. We were welcome to have soft drinks and anything else on sale such as peanuts and chocolate. He wished us good luck with our course and went into the dining room.

We went into the bar and it was quite a shock for most of us to see how smart it was, with a lush carpet and wood panelling. There was even a barman. We ordered soft drinks, paid for on a cash-only basis, and then moved into the dining room next door. Another shock for most of us - tablecloths, crockery, cutlery and table napkins were laid out. There were menus and two waiters in white uniforms. Quite a change from Llewellin!

1400hrs saw us outside Taungup. The senior intake had explained that it was one of a series of lecture rooms at the bottom of a small hill to the east of the camp. Taungup was a battle in the Burma campaign of the Second World War. Lecture rooms were named after battles and barrack rooms after famous commanders. It was interesting to note that despite the fact that Rhodesia had declared itself a republic in 1970, hence severing ties with the UK, no attempt had been made to change these names and the obvious connection with the British military. They remained the same throughout the war. The Royal prefix that some Rhodesian units had been granted post Second World War was reluctantly dropped however.

Colour Wales duly arrived and took us into the lecture room. He sat us down and explained that when the lecturer entered the room we were to brace up. This consisted of us sitting, very upright, with our fists, palms down, on the desk and our arms straight. It was considered a waste of time and too noisy to stand.

"Squad! Squad shun!" We all braced up.

Major Pelham, OC Cadet Wing entered the room. He was also an SAS man. He looked at us for a few seconds. "At ease gentlemen", he said. That was the first time we had been called gentlemen. He went on to give a rough outline of what our course would be like and what would be expected of us.

We would be given batmen employed by the Army, one between three recruits. Their task was to do the washing and ironing of military kit only. Woe betide anyone who got the batman to polish boots or belts or clean brasses. We would be allowed to get the batmen to purchase things for us in town, but we would have to tip them if we did this. It all seemed very civilised.

For the first phase we would double everywhere, either as a squad or as individuals. Each week there would be appointed a duty student who would oversee all movement, organize the drawing of rations and equipment and have command of the squad. He would also be responsible for any group "cock ups".

We were each handed two documents, "Cadet Wing Policy and Standing Orders for Regular and National Service Cadets" and "National Service Cadets' Mess Rules". These were to be regularly referred to.

At the end of the lecture we were doubled to our barrack room. Pete Addison, the first duty student, gave the commands. Our batmen were waiting for us outside the barrack room. Mine turned out to rejoice in the name of Honesty. He turned out to be a character with a very cheerful demeanour and he and other batmen kept our gear in good order. Charlie Lenegan remembers his batman, Arthur, with much affection.

For the rest of the evening we were to work on our kit and clean the barrack room out. We swept and polished and scrubbed until we put the lights out at 2230hrs, with a short break for a drink in the bar and a quick supper.

Tuesday 17 April

Breakfast was at 0630hrs, then back to the barrack room for settling in routine, a euphemism for more cleaning and polishing.

At 0900hrs Colour Wales arrived and off we went for a course photograph. We were told that this photo would be put up on the Cadet Wing noticeboard so that we could be identified by all at School of Infantry.

We were never given copies of this photograph, and as far as I know there was only one. Somehow Pete Addison managed to get a copy. He has no recollection of how he obtained it. All

I can surmise is that he or someone else clandestinely purloined it from Cadet Wing. I saw an electronic copy, made by Charlie Lenegan, for the first time in 2013 while I was writing this account.

It is quite an amusing photograph. We had only been in the Army for six days when it was taken. We do not look at all military but we do look a little bit shattered. At that stage we were wondering what was to come next.

Then it was off to have TAB inoculations to be given in the least-used arm. We found out why after a few hours.

We then moved off to the Q Store to be issued with a knife, fork and spoon, tin mug, mess tins, one rifle cleaning kit, one rifle sling, web belt, webbing, two water bottles, four ammo pouches, one kidney pouch, one pack, a first field dressing, a camouflage face veil, a steel helmet with net covering, a plastic sheet with eyelets, one poncho, one sleeping bag and a panga (machete) in a sheaf. All this took some time.

After lunch we had a lecture by WO2 Hartman on Standing Orders. This covered every move that we were allowed and not allowed to make.

Following this, we had an hour in the barrack room practising getting into the various forms of army dress. Stick kit for the Drill Square, full battle-dress, weapon training order, denim order (with stick-belt, we would only be allowed to wear the stable belt at the end of first phase) and PT kit.

With the stick kit we had been extremely fortunate. At that

particular time there had been a shortage of ankle puttees in the Army and we had not been issued with them. Colour Wales decided that for drill we would therefore forsake the khaki drill shorts and wear denim longs with leggings and stick boots. I secretly blessed him for this. Those without military experience had no idea just how lucky they were.

Memories of putting on the dreaded puttees, with the legendary one eighth of an inch folds, were not happy ones for me, either in cadets or at Gwelo in 1967! I had never seemed to get it right. Sergeant Basil Lentner's voice echoed over the years.

"Sanderson, you scruffy bastard, your folds are anything between half and a quarter of an inch! You're on shine parade!"

We were then shown bed layout. It was not as stringent as I remembered it in 1967 but still enough to take time.

We then had rugby practice. The strangest thing about sport in the Army was that on the sports field everybody was on Christian name terms. It was quite usual to be screamed at by an NCO on the parade ground in the morning only to call him Dennis or Brian or whatever during sports training.

After a long hard practice and fitness training session we were pretty exhausted. Our arms were aching with the after-effects of the TAB injections and we hadn't had a lot of sleep. We slowly wended our way back to the barracks for a shower and then after a quick supper worked until 0130hrs in anticipation of our first morning inspection.

Wednesday 18 April

We got up at 0500hrs to the sound of the "Big Ben Repeater" alarm clock that someone had brought with him. We got our kit laid out and got into drill kit. The trickiest bit of the inspection was the bed pack. Sheets and blanket had to be folded to be absolutely square. We had been told to sleep between the sheets and then assemble the bed pack in the morning before inspection.

We only just managed to put some semblance of an orderly barrack room together before doubling across to breakfast at 0630hrs. Inspection was at 0650hrs, which meant we had to gobble our meal and dash back to be on time. This was to be the pattern for all of first phase. Not much time to luxuriate in our well-appointed mess facility!

The first inspection was a disaster. There was a litany of supposed faults. Colour Wales let rip.

"I want your bed and bed packs square. Your dress is shit. Tuck your bloody shirts in properly. You look like bloody mealie sacks. There is enough dirt on the floors in the barrack room and the toilet block to plant a fucking crop! If you present yourselves like this again, I'll put the whole fucking lot of you gobshites on a charge!" "Gobshites", Charlie Lenegan recalls, was Colour Wales' favourite noun.

From bitter experience, I had been expecting something like this. From experience also, I knew that very often NCOs would find fault with things that in fact were perfectly all right. I was sure the barrack room and toilet block were quite passable. It was just a case of "sticking things out" until the end of first phase. We formed up outside and doubled down to the Drill Square.

For the next three hours we drilled, with two ten-minute spells for "smoke break". Only John Richardson, Tollie Wade and Pete Nupen smoked. We covered, with a great deal of repetition, standing to attention, standing at ease and standing easy, forming up in three ranks, dressing and turning and inclining at the halt. We soon learnt that the trick with drill was not to be noticed, which meant holding concentration to avoid making mistakes.

Then at 0950hrs we had a half-hour break for morning tea. This consisted of a dash to the mess for either tea or a welcome cool drink from the bar. Then we doubled up to Taungup for a lecture.

We braced up at our desks for Captain Boswell of the Pay Corps. He issued us with pay documents and explained the TF (Territorial Force) pay rates and procedures for pay parades. Our pay was to be a dollar a day, calculated from 12 April, and our first pay day was to be 25 April. This was not too good for those of us that had no money. I was all right but a few blokes were very short of cash.

Just before lunch we met our Course Officer, Lieutenant McDermott, for the first time. He was from the Rhodesia African Rifles, the only regular African infantry regiment, based in Bulawayo and at that time consisting of a single battalion. The first thing he did was set us an essay to write, entitled "My Early

Life", due in the next Tuesday – shades of Sir Winston Churchill! We then began an introduction to map reading.

After lunch, we were shown three black and white films, "Bless Them All", "Map Reading Part 1" and "The Infantryman". I remembered seeing them in 1967 but judging by the state of the films they had been around a lot longer than that. It was a particularly cunning move on the part of the military to show films to dog-tired recruits just before or after lunch, especially as it was an offence to go to sleep. All part of the process to break you down before building you up!

To finish the day, we got into PT kit for a physical assessment consisting of a 100-yard sprint (School of Infantry had not as yet gone metric it seemed), press ups, sit ups, climbing ropes, chin ups and a mile run, up to the turn-off on the Gwelo-Bulawayo road and back.

We were all still stiff from our TAB injections and yesterday's rugby practice but were still only in bed by midnight. We left our beds all set up and, using the Army issue sleeping bags, sneakily slept in the empty barrack room next door, hoping that Thursday's inspection would be a little more successful than Wednesday's.

Thursday 19 April

Inspection after breakfast was much better, with a few minor "peeves". Then we were onto the Drill Square to do saluting to the front and dressing in open and close order and then off to Taungup for map reading to learn about grid references, northings, eastings and conventional signs. On the regulation 1:50 000 scale map used by the Rhodesian Army, grid squares were 2 cm by 2 cm, representing 1 km by 1 km. A six-figure grid reference would therefore pinpoint a position to the nearest 100 m.

This was followed up by two short films on map reading re-iterating what we had just covered and then three more on field craft about movement, judging distance and target indication, none of which had yet been covered.

After lunch, now in weapon training order, with camouflage cap replacing beret, combat boots replacing stick boots and webbing, without pack and kidney pouch, replacing the stick belt, we had our first lesson in field craft. The topic was judging distance from the top of the kopje (a rocky hill) on the eastern side of the camp.

We were told that, up to 400 yards, a good method was to try and judge how many units of 100 yards could fit between you and the target. With practice, a quick judgment could be made, bearing in mind that things seem closer on a bright day, when they are bigger than their surroundings, when there is dead ground between and when they are higher. Things seem further on a dull day, when they are smaller than their surroundings, when looking down a road or valley, when they are lower and when lying down.

Then back to Taungup, where we were given our first lesson on weapon training and introduced to the FN, a Belgian-designed counterpart to the SLR (self-loading rifle) which was the British version. The Rhodesian Army had used the SLR until the late sixties, when it became impossible to obtain supplies because of sanctions.

Colour Wales explained that the FN could fire 600 rounds per minute on automatic fire or, when on rapid fire, a round would go off every time the trigger was depressed. The FNs issued at School of Infantry had no bar on the fire selection mechanism, which meant that automatic fire could be selected. However, it was made very clear to us that we would be on a charge if we ever fired on automatic. Most FNs issued elsewhere could only be fired on rapid. Its calibre was 7.62mm, firing intermediate rounds. The Communist AK47 had the same calibre but smaller rounds. The FN muzzle velocity was 2780 ft per second, it weighed 9 pounds and a magazine held 20 rounds. An FN was passed around for us to look at and Colour Wales talked about its operation.

There was no rugby practice because of the coming long Easter weekend; everyone who could wanted to take off for leave straight after work. We, the junior course, were not allowed leave for the first six weeks and were to stay in the camp and be given chores to do. We consoled ourselves with the fact that we would have no inspections for four days and could sleep in with breakfast at 0730hrs.

Friday 20 April

We were fast asleep in the barrack room at 0100hrs when a drunk in denim order stormed into our barrack room and made us all get out of bed and stand to attention. We could see no rank, as he was wearing a combat jacket, but he looked old enough to be at least a Sergeant and this was after all School of Infantry.

"You bastards don't know you are bloody born! There are men out there fighting and dying while you lie in your bloody wank-pits snoring. I'm a sergeant and the thought that I might have to salute one of you little pricks makes me puke! Just jack your bloody selves up!"

With that he turned and left, leaving us half asleep and wondering what it was all about. We found out, a few days later, that he had recently lost a mate in the war and had been drowning his sorrows in the Sergeant and Warrant Officers' Mess all night.

We had no difficulty in getting back to sleep and had a lovely "lie in" until 0700hrs and then a leisurely breakfast before starting a little bit of work on our kit.

During the course so far we had gleaned a bit of information about each other and with a completely undisturbed day, apart from short interruptions for tea and meals, we chatted and got to know each other a little better. In the afternoon a small group of us went for a run to the range via back roads within the camp.

Pete Addison, ex-Prince Edward, had a degree in Engineering and was very fit - a bit of a distance runner.

"Beefy" Barlow, ex-Milton, was an Articled Clerk and very good front row forward. He turned out to be an extremely cheerful soul to have about the place.

Graham Birch, ex-Prince Edward, there during my time, was also a good rugby player.

Mike Evans, ex-Que Que, was a keen military historian but was ill in hospital at this time.

Billy Green, ex-Milton, was already a great reliever of tensions with his dry sense of humour. It had also become clear that on the rugby field he was a fierce tackler and brilliant in cover defence.

Charlie Lenegan, ex-Milton, had a BSc (Economics) from UR (University of Rhodesia) and was also an Articled Clerk.

Keith Lindsay was the "brain" of the course with two degrees.

Rob Mutch, ex-Milton, was a teacher like me. He was another comedian, and he had us in stitches with his Snoopy imitations.

Digby Neuhoff, ex-Plumtree, had a BA from Natal and was teaching at Sinoia.

Pete Nupen, John Richardson, an Irishman, Tollie Wade, ex Oriel, and myself made up the squad. Our average age was 22, higher than usual for a national service officers' course.

We had been left to our own devices all day and went to

bed quite early hoping that we would be left alone the whole weekend.

Saturday 21 April

After another leisurely breakfast we arrived in dribs and drabs at the barrack room to find Colour Wales waiting for us. He gave us a set of chores for the day – no doubt "idle hands" and all that

We were to chop wood into respectable size bits for a braai at the Sergeants and Warrant Officers' Mess, then we were to paint everything around the barrack room that was red (A Company colours), blue (B Company colours). This latter task would take us quite a while, as an awful lot of things were red. A small pot of paint and a couple of brushes were conveniently provided.

We were also told to change the motto that was spelled out, in red, on small stones on a piece of ground just outside the door and that it had to be in Latin. We chose "Mens sana in corpore sano" (A healthy mind in a healthy body).

This took us until well after lunch. At about 1600hrs Colour Wales arrived and presented the course with a bottle of Muscatel in return for chopping the wood – very civilised of him. The alcohol ban being temporarily waived, we tucked into it after supper, out of tin mugs. We got almost a mouthful each!

The rest of the afternoon and evening was spent working on the essay we had been given to write. It had to be 2000 words. Were there that many words? I also dashed off a few letters to various friends dotted about Rhodesia.

Sunday 22 April

The first part of the day of rest was spent building a path, about 40 m long, to the block that housed the room in which I had stayed last time I was at Gwelo, six years previously. The 1967 Regular Officers Cadets were housed in a block, with one cadet to each room right at the beginning of the course. Apparently at that stage there were no barrack rooms available.

We drew picks and shovels from the Quartermaster's Store, obligingly opened just for us, and worked with bricks, sand and gravel, already in piles, to complete the task.

The afternoon was spent clearing dead leaves and weeding garden beds outside Cadet Wing. Helping us was a Private Diamond, another Prince Edward old boy from my time teaching there. He had been in the regulars for some two years and was on a charge over some misdemeanour, "slumming it" with the national servicemen Officer Cadets.

We were "the lowest of the low". This had been made clear to us at an emotional moment during drill on Thursday. Colour Wales had been more than put out by the way we were doing close and open order dressing.

"You lot are the sloppiest gobshites I have ever seen! Typical Officer Cadets, totally bloody useless! Officer Cadets are the lowest rank in the whole fucking Rhodesian Army so I shouldn't be bloody surprised! You pricks are lower than shark shit!"

The philosophy behind the last allusion was that sharks often swam along the bottom of the sea and so, logically, their droppings would be deposited there without having to sink. Colour Sergeants had many choice phrases, which they trotted out more to alleviate their boredom than for any other reason.

We had been kept busy all day and with a major inspection due on Tuesday, we were hoping for some time on Easter Monday to work on our barrack room and kit.

Monday 23 April

We were left alone on Monday. We spent some time cleaning and polishing the barrack room and adjacent washroom, which needed quite a bit of work. We managed to filch a polisher from the kitchen. Electrolux made it all much easier.

There was time for reflection and a bit of letter writing. I dashed off a missive to Russell Williams of Parks and Wildlife, a friend of mine in Kariba. Unfortunately, Russell was killed in action on 12 January 1978.

At School of Infantry on courses 129 and 130 were another three Prince Edward old boys, "DAB" Kenny, Tim Henwood and Lewis Hartley, all of whom had been at the school in my time. I wondered idly if any of them would get commissioned and I would have to salute them.

So far, as a course, we were happy with how things were going. Colour Wales didn't seem to be too big on the Army bullshit handed out by some instructors, which we appreciated. We seemed as a course to be getting on reasonably well and to be getting the hang of things quite easily.

We had come up with the ingenious idea of putting our bed pack, already set up, "boxed" with pieces of stiff plywood to get it square, in our trunks overnight. Most of us had acquired an extra sheet to give the impression that we were sleeping as per instructions. It was simply a case of stretching a blanket over the bed and then setting things up.

We had an early night, getting to bed at 2130hrs.

Tuesday 24 April

We were up at 0430hrs to get our beds ready. Then, at 0530hrs, we had a PT session taken by Lieutenant McDermott, one of the most strenuous I had ever had. We doubled around the rugby field several times in the faint dawn light then ran to the top of the hill next to the road leading out of School of Infantry, where there was a reservoir. Then we ran back, a distance of about 1 km.

We then embarked on a game of rugby with a huge log as the ball. There were no rules; the object was to get the log over the try line, starting with the log on the ground at the centre of the field. We divided into two groups and set to. Eventually, after much pushing, shoving and tackling men with or without the log, one of the teams pushed it over a try line and grounded it.

"Right", screamed Lieutenant McDermott, "Take the log back to the centre and start again".

We picked it up took it back to the centre line and dropped it. Our Course Officer went ballistic.

"Don't drop my fucking log! Pick it up and put it down gently."

This torment went on until 0715hrs, when we were released, most of us on our knees, for a lightning shower, a change into drill kit and a late breakfast with instructions to be ready for a barrack room inspection at 0800hrs. We all fared a little better this time, with a limited number of derogatory comments from Colour Wales, and then we were off to the Drill Square to do numbering (each of us loudly calling out a number starting with one along each rank) and compliments. The latter consisted of practising the salute about 100 times.

We handed in our essays and were then shown the remaining three films on map reading and given a practical on measuring distances and bearings on a map. We also had to know the difference between grid north and magnetic north. For the compass variation in Rhodesia in 1973, we were given the easy to remember mnemonic "grid to mag, add, mag to grid, get rid".

After lunch we had weapon training. We doubled down to the armoury and we each drew and signed for an FN. It was made very clear to us by the Quartermaster Sergeant that the rifle would be well cleaned before it was handed back and that any departure from proceedings would result in dire consequences.

The first part of the lesson was stripping the rifle and the "naming of parts". We then practised the load and unload with drill rounds. We learned that when cocking, the mechanism had to be released under its own steam. Most of us made the potentially fatal mistake of pushing the cocking handle back after the initial cocking, resulting in a jammed round. Colour Wales had to "unjam" the rifles by pushing the cocking handle open with a trust of his foot with the admonishment "You'd look fucking stupid if this happened in a bloody contact, wouldn't you?"

We returned our rifles after stripping and cleaning them with our rifle cleaning kits on a huge well-worn wooden table outside the Q-Store.

The day finished with more field-craft, namely the identification of targets to enable fire to be brought down on them. We took it in turns to identify targets given to us by our instructor, for the rest of the group.

There were three methods of doing this. The direct method was used to indicate obvious targets, for example "300, half right, lone bush (target)". The reference point method was used for less obvious targets, for example "300, bushy topped tree (reference point), slightly right – small bush (target)".

The clock ray method was used for even less obvious targets, for example "300, windmill (reference point regarded as at 12 o'clock from your position), 2 o'clock – small hut (target)".

The physical day ended with a one-and-a-half-hour rugby session, consisting entirely of match practice, leaving us drained as we went back to our barrack room to clean and polish.

Wednesday 25 April

We were waiting for inspection at 0700hrs, but Colour Wales was late and took us straight to the Drill Square. Again we got the impression that he was not big on the regulation army bullshit. We revised what we had already done and learnt the side pace, then off to Taungup for the first lesson on Voice Procedure, basically the procedure for coping with radio communications.

The first and major emphasis was on security. Apparently during the Second World War 80% of all intelligence was acquired as a result of listening to enemy radio traffic. Apparently, also, the Allies had broken the German Enigma code and for a long time the Germans had no idea that this breach of security had occurred.

We were told that we had our own system of coding, namely shackle, slidex and plackard, and that all radio communications (comms) were to be carried out using this when giving out information that could be useful to the enemy, such as position as a grid reference. Only in the event of a contact was a message to be sent in clear. For communications with one's own unit, previously made-up nicknames, report lines, code words and veiled speech could be used. Codes would be contained in a document called a scant list.

It was also vital to have accuracy and economy in a radio message. Numbers had to be given digit by digit, to be preceded by the word "figures" except in the case of call signs and time checks. If a word had to be spelled out the standard NATO phonetic alphabet was to be used, preceded by the phrase "I spell".

Economy would involve correct use of pro-words as proscribed by the Rhodesian Army. For example "fetch Sunray" would be used instead of "go and get the commander of your unit". "Sunray" was the appointment title for the person in charge of any unit of whatever size. We were given a list of appointment titles.

Overall discipline consisted of correct use of voice procedure, closing down and opening up stations, use of correct frequency and constant radio watch.

Finally we had a session on radio nets with numerous examples from battalion level downwards. For example, HQ A Company would have call sign 1, HQ B Company would have call sign 2 and so on. Number one platoon and number two platoon in A Company would have call signs 11 and 12 respectively. Number one and number two sections in number one platoon in A Company would have call signs 11A and 11B respectively.

After lunch we had a pay parade. We lined up outside the pay office and marched in one by one, saluted the officer signed for the pay and marched out again. We were given the princely sum of $15.21, some of it an advance, for two weeks' work!

Wednesday afternoons were for sport and we whiled away the time with a two-hour game of basketball before the usual evening routine of studying (we were to learn the phonetic alphabet), polishing and cleaning.

So far I had managed to write something in my diary every day, although finding time to do so was sometimes difficult. A couple of blokes were showing a bit of interest in it even offering suggestions as to content. All contributions were gratefully received.

Thursday 26 April

Once again we were up at 0430hrs to get the barrack room ready and then off to a PT session, this time at 0600hrs. We were introduced to "log runs". Groups of four (there were now 12 of us with Mike Evans still in hospital) each carried a gum log on their shoulders at the double up the hill to the reservoir and back. Then we went again and again. In all we did it four times.

The problem with "log runs" was that people were of different heights and so were their shoulders! The two tallest in each group were placed at the ends with the log on their shoulders and the two shortest in the middle.

Colour Wales, displaying lower reptilian cunning, selected the groups with two tall and two not so tall people in them. The shorter pair could not rest the log on their shoulders and were supposed to hold it up with their hands. Well, try doing that for several kilometres. Cries of "Hold the bloody log up!" and "We can't, our arms are too tired!" echoed up and down the hill for the entire PT session.

We lurched off to breakfast and did a lightning change into weapon training order for another lesson on field craft. We went to the top of the hill above the lecture rooms to practise target indication and to learn fire orders.

We were given acronyms to remember things. For fire orders, we used CLAP, which caused a certain amount of amusement, and GRIT. CLAP stood for clear, loud, as an order and with pauses. GRIT stood for group, range, indication and type of fire.

When we had finished, Colour Wales made us race down the hill, complete with pointer staffs, to see who would be the last man outside the C/Sgt's hut. I was just coming out of the bush when something occurred to me. I said to the bloke behind me "How is Wales going to know who the last man is without running down the hill himself?"

Unfortunately, the bloke behind me turned out to be Colour Wales, running down the hill himself. To my relief he just laughed.

Map reading was next on the agenda. We took grid bearings, using service protractors, converted them to magnetic bearings and measured distances between points on the map.

The afternoon was spent on weapon training with the FN. We worked on aiming and firing, simulated of course. The instructor would hold a small round white disc with a hole in the middle and look through it. We would aim the rifle to hit the small hole. The instructor would be able to see if our sights were lined up correctly.

When simulating the firing, the drill round, of course, would not go off and so the firing mechanism would not be forced back by the expanding gases and we would have to cock the rifle ourselves.

Once again every now and then we would forget to allow the mechanism, after cocking, to return under its own steam and a round would jam and each time Colour Wales would have a sense of humour failure. "The terrs will have you pricks for their bloody breakfast," we would be told.

At 1700hrs we were off to rugby practice and after spending the evening cleaning, studying code words, appointment titles and call signs for voice procedure we collapsed into bed at 2300hrs.

Friday 27 April

The two-hour drill session, at 0700hrs, incorporated marching and halting in quick time and getting on parade, the latter in preparation for our first musters parade in about a week's time. It wasn't a huge success. Colour Wales and half the course had bad colds and our concentration was not at its best. However, we muddled through and moved onto voice procedure.

We covered types of call, namely single calls, multiple calls, collective calls and all stations calls. Each type of call, except the all stations call, involved stating the relevant call signs at the beginning of each transmission. We moved onto establishing communication on a simple net. Once again this involved the use of call signs and proscribed pro-words.

We then covered offering messages and how to cope with corrections and repetitions, once again using specific pro-words. For example the pro-words "Long message, ready to copy?" were followed by the message, broken down into parts, with the acknowledgement request, "Did you copy?" after each part was given. The reply could be, as an example, "Affirmative, go," or "Negative. Say again all after...."

We were informed that quaint American, Boys' Own or "Biggles" type phrases such as "wilco", "chocks away chaps", "copied" and "OK" were extremely frowned upon.

After lunch we moved onto weapon training. We drew weapons and went to Taungup for a lecture on the mechanism of the FN, complete with cross-sectional diagrams.

As the rifle is fired, gas escapes through a small hole in the top of the barrel into a gas chamber. This gas, the amount controlled by a manually set gas regulator, pushes the gas piston back, which in turn pushes the breech-block back to eject the empty cartridge and bring a new one into the chamber. A strong spring in the butt forces the breech-block back (together with the gas piston) and the whole process is then repeated.

We then moved to the weapon training area and practised dealing with stoppages. There were several different types and we practiced them all. We lay in the prone position for the drills, on stony ground, so the skin on our elbows slowly wore away as time went on.

Colour Wales, not feeling too well, was in fine form. "You are firing! Your rifle stops!" This meant that when you pulled the trigger nothing happened.

"Cock, hook and look!" This meant that you should cock the rifle, hook back the mechanism and look to see what was causing the stoppage.

"Empty magazine!" At this we were supposed to take the magazine off the rifle and replace it with a new one.

"You are firing! Your rifle stops! Cock hook and look! Round caught in firing mechanism!" At this we had to remove the magazine, pretend to clear the round and replace the magazine.

"You are firing! Your rifle stops! Cock hook and look! Round has not ejected!" At this we had to remove the magazine, pretend to eject the spent cartridge case and check the gas regulator before replacing the magazine.

We wound up the afternoon practising moving with and without rifles, mostly, once again, in the prone position. By the end of the session our elbows were rubbed raw.

We were new to these tasks and made plenty of mistakes. We shuffled off to the armoury to clean and hand in our weapons with the none-too-complimentary comments of our instructor echoing in our ears: "You gungy bastards had better jack yourselves up the next time we do weapon training!"

We spent the evening getting ready for our first big Saturday morning inspection, to be taken by Colour Sergeant Wales.

Saturday 28 April

Colour Wales was ill, so our inspection was taken by Colour Sergeant van Rensburg, who turned out to be our inebriated mystery post-midnight visitor of a few days back. He was a different kettle of fish from our regular instructor. He obviously believed in shine parades. "Your barrack room is not too bad, just a few little things to fix up. There will be another inspection at 1930hrs tonight!"

We then had two hours' drill, revising all we had done and incorporating saluting on the march. We then doubled off to Moyale, a different lecture room, for another lecture on voice procedure while Colour Sergeant van Rensburg took a smoke break.

We were waylaid by Regimental Sergeant Major Collyer, a dangerous figure that we had heard of and had seen marching around the place in the middle distance with a pace stick under his arm. So far he had left us alone, presumably because we were so bad that we were below his dignity. Today, however, he decided to pay us a little attention. A huge bellow reached across the hundred metres between him and us.

"Halt that squad!"

Our duty student obliged and we stood nervously to attention. He marched up to us.

"You wanked-out pimply-faced youths should have been strangled at birth! You, you gungy bastard, what's your name?" The latter remark was addressed to Billy Green.

"Green, Sergeant Major!" Most of us gasped inwardly at this huge gaffe and waited for the inevitable explosion.

There was a pregnant pause.

RSM Collyer brought his face right up to Billy's ear.

"What did you say?" he asked softly.

Billy compounded his error. "Green, Sergeant Major!" this time shouting it out even louder.

This was too much for the RSM. "You horrible little youth", he screamed, "you call me sir; do you understand? Sir!"

Billy kept his head although we could see he was getting very angry. "Yes, sir", he screamed.

RSM Collyer seemed to tire of Billy and turned his attention on the squad.

"When you move as a squad keep in step. You looked like a bloody herd of cattle. If you double like that again, I'll put the whole lot of you on a charge! Carry on."

We doubled off, feeling that we had got off lightly.

Voice procedure consisted of a revision of what we had done so far and verifying, cancelling and acknowledging long transmissions. It was important to break long messages up into segments, once again using correct pro-words.

In the afternoon were the first rugby games of the season, at School of Infantry. As the junior squad we had to carry the stands from the basketball court to the rugby field, a distance of about 250 metres, run the gate, man the scoreboard, run the cool-drink stand and supply touch judges. In addition some of us had to play a game of rugby for the First or Second Teams against Gwelo Sports Club.

Watching the game were two teaching colleagues of mine, Bill Baker and Selwyn Stevens, both teaching at Chaplin. Bill's rugby team had been playing the curtain raiser. I managed only a snatched conservation with them between duties.

We staggered back to our barrack room to get ready for our shine parade. Remembering how sticky some NCOs could be about shaving and expecting trouble, I had a second shave, anything to avoid a "nause" (short for nausea, Army slang for a disaster). We then stood by our beds with full kit layout and waited the arrival of Colour van Rensburg. By 2000hrs, we realised that he was not going to arrive and spent the rest of the evening studying for our first progress test due on Tuesday. We also had project work to do. Charlie Lenegan and I had to research the topic "The formation of the earth" and present a lecture on the subject. It turned out that we never did have to present the lecture, despite all our work.

Sunday 29 April

We had a leisurely lie-in until 0730hrs, as with last weekend, a luxury almost undreamed of, and a slow breakfast. Most of the day was spent studying for Tuesday's progress test, writing letters and the inevitable kit cleaning and polishing.

We took a long break for morning tea. This was supplied every day in the mess, normally straight after drill, but we very seldom took advantage of it as we were always in such a rush. At best we would grab a coke and a packet of crisps or a "flakie" from the bar and move on rapidly. It was good to be able to spend some time relaxing.

The bar, as well as being well appointed, had a stereo in one of the corners. At the time there was only one record available, "Teaser and the Fire-cat" by Cat Stevens. This particular recording was, needless to say, played to death. To this day "Morning has Broken" and "Moonshadow" bring back a flood of memories of my time at School of Infantry.

We got the news that one of our original number, Mike Evans, who had been ill for the last ten days, had been "RTU'ed". This stood for "Returned to Unit" meaning, in our case, returning to Llewellin Barracks. We as a course thought that this was a bit unfair as we felt that Mike could have caught up on what we had done so far, but the Army did not seem to think so. We wondered how many more of us would suffer the same fate before the end of the course.

Monday 30 April

We were up at 0530hrs and ready for inspection, after breakfast at 0655hrs. Colour Wales was late and so inspection was very quick and we moved off to the Drill Square. We covered turnings and inclinings in quick time. I was made right hand marker, which meant that I would be the first to get on parade at musters and get screamed at by the RSM.

Half way through our drill we left the Drill Square and formed up on the side to watch our first muster parade.

The squads, 129, 130, two squads of African demonstration troops and one squad of RAR troops on a mortar course, formed up on the opposite edge of the square facing regimental wing. The Regimental Sergeant Major came out of his office and paced about the regimental wing edge of the square opposite the squads, glaring at them every now and then and generally looking ominous.

After about a minute, he came to attention, with his pace stick under his arm, marched to the middle of the square and halted. A huge roar reached our ears.

"Right, markers!"

At this, the right hand marker, the man in each squad at the end of the front rank, began marching onto the square a designated number of paces. They came to a halt and stood rigidly to attention.

Another roar issued from the RSM.

"Get on parade!"

The remainder of the squads began marching onto the square to join the right markers.

"Dressing! Right dress!"

This was the signal for the squads to get in line and at the correct distance apart. After much shuffling, this was achieved. There was a silent pause, the calm before the storm. RSM Collyer surveyed the parade with total distain, as if he could not believe his eyes. He zeroed in on a chubby little Sergeant Major in charge of one of the African squads.

"You grubby individual, your squad is a total disgrace! Your drill is shit, your dress is shit and you are sloppy! You had better jack yourself up before I put you on a charge!"

The RSM moved on, delivering the odd comment, and then seemed to tire of the proceedings and marched the squads off the square. This was done at a ridiculous pace, with RSM Collyer shouting the time.

"Left, right, left, right, pick your bloody feet up!"

We found it hard not to start laughing. It all looked quite comical. I couldn't help thinking that the whole process could have been done better.

After drill we moved to Taungup for Map Reading. We learnt about fixing a position by finding back bearings from prominent landmarks to intersect at one's position.

Our Course Officer was away and so we had Lieutenant MacDonald for lectures. I made the mistake of yawning and wound up doubling five times around the lecture room to "wake me up".

We recognized Lieutenant MacDonald as a fine soldier. He had received the Sword of Honour in the 1968/1969 regular officers' course.

After our customary dash to the bar for a quick cool drink we moved on to voice procedure, covering changing frequency, closing down, assuming control of a net, joining a working net and giving time signals.

Each procedure, as usual, had its own special pro-words and once again any deviation from these was frowned upon. It was explained that a very accurate time signal was necessary so that units acting in a coordinated operation would all act on cue with previously planned timings. For instance, it would be no use if an artillery smoke barrage, designed to provide cover to advancing infantry and due to begin at 0612hrs, actually started at 0613hrs.

In the afternoon we had three hours of weapon training on the FN. We learnt about elevation and wind adjustments.

At 200m, adjusting the sight one notch allowed a drop or rise of six inches on the MPI (mean point of impact). The figures for 300m and 400m were 12 inches and 18 inches respectively. For example, if we were 400m from the target and had our sights set at 300m, we could expect our rounds to fall 18 inches below our aiming point or if we were 300m from the target and had our sights set at 400m, we could expect our rounds to be 12 inches higher than our point of aim.

The wind had to be judged as mild, fresh or strong and there were complicated sets of adjustment rules to cater for the effect of wind. With experience, we found that lots of practice was the best way of handling wind adjustment.

For once, we managed to get an hour or so in the bar after supper, all of us religiously sticking to soft drinks, but a pleasant interlude none the less. It was at times like this that we could get to know each other a little better. After a barrack room clean and studying a little more for Tuesday's progress test we fell into bed at 2230hrs.

Tuesday 1 May

We were up at 0500hrs and waiting, in PT kit, at the start of the assault course at 0600hrs. Our instructor went through the various ways of negotiating the more awkward barriers and then off we went. The course took about 4 minutes and we did it five times. We staggered off to shower and have our breakfast before barrack room inspection.

Colour Wales had determined on a very rigorous inspection this time round. All of us got a "rev" whether we deserved it or not.

"Wade, you are a horrible excuse for a soldier!"

"Lindsay, your bed space is shit!"

Every now and then there was a touching display of humour.

"Green, you've got mosquito shit all over your leggings!"

Then off we went to the Drill Square to do marking time, marking time off the march and moving forward again, halting off the mark time and changing step in quick time.

Each time we would fall in on the Drill Square and practise what we had already learnt. Then we would be introduced to the new drill, always with the preliminary, "This movement is taught to you to enable you as an individual or as a body of men to ....."

We moved off to Taungup to do our first progress test. It was very stiff, with an awful lot of questions in the one hour available.

Next was voice procedure. Lieutenant McDermott was away again so we had Staff Sergeant Stoltz, from Signals, who took us through authentication, use of the shackle code and NIS (net identification signs).

Just after lunch we had a film on camouflage and concealment followed by a lengthy practical session in the training area. Faces had to be black with camouflage cream, burnt cork or mud, smeared for night work streaked for the day. The rest of the body was to have grass and small green branches pushed in buttonholes, webbing and boots.

During most of the Rhodesian War many of our troops would operate in shorts with little effort at camouflage. Later in the war, captured terrorists told us that this was often a dead giveaway and towards the end of the war troops moved in the camouflage long trousers.

For concealment we were to use shadows, choose a background to match our camouflage, avoid isolated cover and observe around cover, not over the top. I often wondered if camouflage and concealment was emphasised strongly enough in basic training. In our entire time at School of Infantry we only spent this one afternoon specifically on personal camouflage and concealment.

The practical was quite frightening. Some of us dispersed into a well-wooded area about 200m by 200m and the rest searched for us. If someone was adequately camouflaged and amongst vegetation, it was very difficult to spot him until you were right on top of him. Many a time men walked right past me, literally a metre away, without seeing me, and the same thing happened to me when I was looking for them.

Rugby practice ended the day.

Wednesday 2 May

The day started with drill, straight onto the square without an inspection, courtesy of Colour Wales. We spent an hour revising everything we had done so far.

In voice procedure we covered relay procedures, repetitions of call signs and read back procedure. For whatever reason, radio communication in Rhodesia was sometimes difficult and it was often impossible to reach the required station. Relay stations would be set up on high ground and messages would be sent via them. Read-back procedure was used to check that stations had received the correct message.

We then moved onto Staff Duties (SD), taken by Major Pelham. This covered all aspects relating to Army staff work. We were to concentrate on service writing, literally how the Army dots the i's and crosses the t's.

We learned that, in all army documents, title headings and main headings would be in the middle. Group headings (like civilian sub-headings) would be on the left hand side. Paragraph headings, if used, would be indented five spaces from the left margin.

If a paragraph heading was not used, paragraphs would be written in block form with the paragraph letter (a, b, c etc) written five spaces in from the left margin. Further sub-division was possible by indentation and the use of Roman numerals (i, ii, iv etc) and even further sub-division by indentation and the use of letters in small brackets ((a), (b), (c) etc).

We were shown the layout of various forms of correspondence such as routine letters, formal letters, demi-official letters, memorandums and service papers. We found it a little bit dull, but all this came in very handy later on when we had finished our basic training and were moved on to our various units.

The morning concluded with revision of map reading in preparation for our tutorial exercise out in the bush due next Thursday.

After lunch we had several runs over the assault course and after that, it being officially the sports afternoon, Colour Wales kindly left us to our own devices. Pete Addison and I went for a run to the range. We were due to go out there on Friday to fire the FN and we wanted another "look see". It was a round trip of about two miles.

We managed to find time for a few drinks (soft) in the mess after dinner but didn't linger too long. We had a feeling that Colour Wales might well do a strict inspection the following morning and our barrack room needed a bit more than a "once over"

Thursday 3 May

The day started with PT. We went a couple of times round the assault course and then had a log run to the top of the kopje and back. We had a late breakfast at 0730hrs and were standing by our beds at 0800hrs having just had enough time to change into denim order as there was no scheduled drill. Colour Wales entered the barrack room. You could see he was "on a mission".

"Squad! Squad shun!" bawled the duty student.

We all came to attention and waited. We all got a "rev". It was going to be that sort of day.

Colour Wales halted by Keith Lindsay's bed and surveyed him disdainfully up and down. However, before he could find fault, he noticed that there was a small ant running around on his bed.

Colour Wales' voice took on almost dulcet tones. "Lindsay", he almost whispered, "are pets allowed in the barrack room?"

"No Colour!" replied the hapless Keith. There was a pause before the inevitable explosion.

"Then what the bloody hell is this animal doing on your fucking bed?"

Colour Wales finished the inspection with a final admonishment. "This barrack room is totally unacceptable! You're all on shine parade at 1900hrs!"

We moved off, slightly irritated, to Taungup for our first lesson on the MAG, the all-purpose machine gun used throughout the Rhodesian Army. This could fire 600, 800 or 1000 rounds per minute, depending on the gas regulator setting. Each belt, consisting of articulated metal links, contained 50 rounds. Belts could be linked for more continuous fire. Its calibre was 7.62mm, the same as the FN. It could be fired from a permanently-attached bipod up to 800m and from a tripod up to 1800m. It was simple to operate, with few stoppages.

After weapon training we moved on to a practical; using radios for the first time, speaking into the voice piece but not switching them on. We soon found out that practice was different from theory. We used A60s, developed and manufactured in South Africa. We were also given a practice scant list for encoding grid references.

We split up into pairs and spoke to each other about 3m apart, so that we could hear each other, putting into practice what we had learned so far. We had to operate off a sheet that we had each been given and which had several designated tasks on it. Colour Wales moved from group to group eavesdropping.

I was with Tollie Wade. My call sign was 11A and Tollie's was 11B. We were representing No.1 and No.2 Sections of No.1 Platoon, A Company.

Things seemed to go well for a while. "Hello one-one bravo, this is one-one alpha, do you read?"

"Hello one-one alpha, this is one-one bravo, fives." The clarity of radio reception was rated from ones, meaning impossible to make out, to fives, meaning totally clear.

Our instructor drifted across to us. We carried on regardless. It was Tollie's turn to send a message.

"One-one alpha, this is one-one bravo, do you read?"

"One-one alpha, fives."

"Ready to copy message."

Wales interjected. "Use your call sign each time you speak, Wade."

Tollie tried again. "One-one bravo, ready to copy message?" And so it went on.

It was my turn to do a contact report. We were told that was one occasion when grid references could be sent in clear and I would not have to encode anything. We were also told that we should preface giving the grid reference of our position with the phrase "contact, contact".

"One-one bravo, this is one-one alpha, contact, contact."

"One-one bravo, go."

"One-one alpha, our position is two seven oh eight six three." I was giving the grid reference. This was not the correct format for a contact report, but we hadn't been taught that yet, so it was totally overlooked. Something more fundamental wasn't overlooked.

Wales was still listening to us, and he exploded. "You don't say oh! Only virgins say oh! You say zero!"

And there, I had thought that I was doing so well. Obviously I was still a long way from being a soldier.

Colour Wales' had a point. Apparently on the radio, with the attendant static, "oh" could sound like "eight" and result in incorrect information being transmitted.

The whole afternoon was spent with the FN, revising everything we had learnt and practising our training tests, in anticipation of our introductory shoot on Friday. We had to pass these before we would be allowed on the range.

The trickiest tests were the loading tests. A magazine held twenty rounds. We had to fill the magazine from clips of five, replace the magazine and cock to load the rifle in 35 seconds. It was a lot more difficult than it sounded.

Rugby practice was hard going. Our coaches had decided that we were not fit enough and went mad! We staggered back to our barrack room exhausted, had a lightning shower, changed into denim order, rushed to the mess for supper and hurtled back to the barrack room for our shine parade.

The duty NCO, who had obviously been briefed about our

unsuccessful morning inspection by Wales, turned out to be none other than Colour Sergeant van Rensburg. Horror of horrors!

Colour van Rensburg marched up and down the barrack room without saying a word. Then he spoke.

"Your kit is not laid out too badly and your uniforms are not too sloppy. You've passed."

We breathed a sigh of relief. Essentially, we couldn't believe that we had been let off so easily. We surmised that he must have won the State Lottery to have put him in such an unusually good mood!

Friday 4 May

For some reason, probably because we were off to the range, we had no inspection or drill and the day started with us drawing weapons, at 0815hrs, followed by training tests. These focused on loading, aiming, adopting various firing positions and running through the gamut of stoppages.

We then moved onto our new lecture room, Moyale, for a lesson on how to mark up maps with military symbols, followed by a talk on military abbreviations. Needless to say we were given a huge revision exercise on military symbols to do over the weekend.

The afternoon was spent with live firing. We climbed aboard an RL with our weapons and a box of live round ammunition and were driven out to the range. We debussed and were briefed on the shoot.

Half of us went to the butts and the rest fired five rounds, from 100 yards, at the regulation target consisting of a life-size picture of the torso of a man. The men in the butts would then haul the target down and record the target number and the size of the grouping, four inch, eight inch or worse. They would then patch the bullet holes with glue and small square bits of paper, black or white to match the pattern of the target. They would then haul the targets up again for the next five rounds. After 15 rounds the men in the butts would change places with the men firing and the procedure would be repeated.

My rifle did not function well and I had a great number of stoppages. The firing mechanism would not automatically reload even on the maximum gas setting and I had to cock the rifle each time I fired. This was my excuse for only getting one four inch grouping, the rest being eight inch.

This earned a neat little compliment from Colour Wales. "Sanderson, your shooting is like a mad woman's shit - all over the place!"

Well, we were warned that the aim was to beat us down to eventually build us up. I began to wonder at which stage the building up would begin. Fortunately I was allowed to draw a different rifle in future, which was in perfect working order, and saw me through my training.

That evening we found a little bit of time for some socialising in the mess.

I read in the orders posted on the notice board outside the mess that I was in the seconds rugby team for the away matches against Risco (Rhodesia Iron and Steel Corporation), near Que

Que on Saturday. This was good news because, as a member of a rugby team, I would be allowed to have a few beers after the match, my first in three weeks.

As usual the last part of the evening was spent preparing for next morning's inspection, the big Saturday one. We all longed for the end of the first phase, in three weeks' time now, and then, hopefully, a little less emphasis on the spit and polish.

Saturday 5 May

According to Colour Wales, when he finished his inspection there were only a few niggling things wrong with our turnout. I personally saw no difference between our turnout today and our turnout when we had the shine parade, but then I have never been "Mr Observant". Colour Wales focused most of his attention on Keith Lindsay, with his two university degrees.

"Lindsay, you may have two degrees but you've still got a shit bed space."

"Yes Colour!"

"What's this gunge doing on your toothbrush?"

"I don't know, Colour!"

"Where have you been putting it?"

"Nowhere, Colour!"

Such sparkling repartee!

We had two hours of drill revising everything and learning how to break into double and quick time. Then after an early lunch we changed into "civvies" and boarded the bus to Risco.

On the way I discovered that a fellow from Intake 130, Laurie Rickards, like myself, was a Gilbert and Sullivan fan and we spent the best part of the journey singing snatches of songs from the various operas, much, I am sure, to the irritation of the other team members. I didn't see anything strange in the situation, although I am sure others did!

After the games we gathered in the Risco Club and I eased into my first drink for a while. I started with a shandy, which didn't touch the sides, then moved onto Castle lager. One of the Sergeants made the comment that drinking Castle was like sex by the seaside - fucking close to water. Just as well, I thought, because I intended to have a few of them!

Our team Captain, Captain Boswell, came over to me.

"I've been wondering where I met you before" he said, "and I've just realised. You were with me, Johnny Dawson and the boys in 1967."

Then I recognised him. It was Vince Boswell, the officer who had given us our first pay. We had been regular Officer Cadets together. We had cleaned our boots together!

"God" I said, "You're all Captains out of that course at School of Infantry and I'm still a bloody rifleman!"

He laughed at this.

The evening progressed as most post-rugby game gatherings do, with flowing booze and bawdy rugby songs. One became a favourite of ours, "The Engineer's Song". Many a time, after a long day, the shower rooms with their superior acoustics would echo to its strains.

The bus left for School of Infantry, but I missed it and cadged a lift with some blokes from the senior intakes to the Midlands Hotel for a few more drinks, a strictly illegal move, before staggering the couple of miles back to School of Infantry. Luckily I got away with it. Technically I could have been "RTU'ed" for this. Still, it had been a great evening.

Sunday 6 May

I should have felt worse than I did on Sunday morning after the previous night's excesses. We spent most of the day working on our extensive military symbols exercise and studying for the second progress test.

The best part of Sundays was that we were left alone. No one was constantly "on our case". There was a chance for a bit of leisure and reflection without being under constant observation.

One of the drawbacks of being on a national service officer's course was the constant possibility of being "RTU'ed". Already I had the feeling that one or two of us were being targeted, having just that little bit more attention being paid to them on the Drill Square, at inspection and elsewhere. All of us copped an individual blast several times a day and we all wondered, at times, if we could be possible candidates for "relegation".

We got the news during the day that Colour Wales would be in Salisbury for the following week and that we would be getting Sergeant Nel from regimental wing as our instructor.

He had been my centre on Saturday with me at fly half giving him instructions on alignment. I certainly would not be giving him instructions in the coming week.

Monday 7 May

We were up at 0600hrs and off for a road run out of the camp and along the Bulawayo road and back. We then grabbed a quick breakfast, had a passable inspection and moved off to muster parade at 0800hrs. The same rigmarole took place but with us joining in for the first time. Fortunately the RSM focused his tirade on the same squad as the previous week and we escaped any major attention.

Everybody left the Drill Square except us. We had drawn weapons and had our first session of arms drill. We covered shouldering arms from the order arms position.

The last time I had done arms drill we were using the SLR (Self Loading Rifle), the British equivalent of the FN. This weapon had a folding over cocking handle on the left and so it was possible to shoulder arms on the right from the order arms on the right. With the FN, however, because the cocking handle protruded, the shoulder arms had to be on the left necessitating a cross over from the order arms position. This made the movement a lot harder. Sergeant Nel was extremely patient with us despite numerous "cock ups".

We moved on to Moyale to hand in our military symbols exercise and have a lecture by Lieutenant McDermott on the organization and roles of the Rhodesian Army. It was to my mind woefully small, basically the equivalent of one small division. It expanded greatly over the next seven years of the war but was never big enough to adequately cope with the defence of such a long border.

For its size, it should have been commanded by a Major General, but possibly in anticipation of this expansion we had a Lieutenant General, Peter Walls, in charge.

The approximate strength at the time was 720 officers (322 regulars) and 11,945 other ranks. Any army can be divided up in several different ways. We were given two ways in which this could be done.

The Rhodesian Army could be divided into Corps, each Corps carrying out mostly specific military tasks within the command structure. The Rhodesian Army in 1973 consisted of 11 Corps: Army Staff Corps, Artillery, Engineers, Signals, Infantry, Chaplains, Service Corps, Medical Corps, Military Police, Pay Corps and Education Corps. All of these had their own insignia and stable belts except the Corps of Infantry, where each unit had its own (Rhodesia Regiment, Rhodesian Light Infantry, Rhodesian African Rifles, Special Air Service and Rhodesian Defence Regiment). Corps could be large or small in numbers from several units of battalion strength, as in the Corps of Infantry, to a few individuals, as in the Corps of Chaplains.

It could also be divided by command structure, on which we were to focus, into four groups, each of which had other sub-divisions, the Static Command (basically the Divisional HQ), Field Force, Administration Service and Training Establishments. Static Command had direct or indirect authority over the other three groups.

The composition of the Field Force, indirectly under Static Command control, as it was in May 1973, is shown below.

The three brigade areas were Matabeleland (1 Brigade), Mashonaland (2 Brigade) and Manicaland (3 Brigade).

DIVISIONAL HQ

No.1 Brigade HQ	No. 2 Brigade HQ	No.3 Brigade HQ
1 Eng.Sqn.	2 Eng.Sqn	3 Eng.Sqn.
1 Bde.Sigs.Sqn	2 Bde.Sigs.Sqn.	4 RR
1 RAR	1 RLI	Detach. RhMP
2 RR	1 RR	
6 RR	5 RR	
9 RR	8 RR	
1 Indep.Coy.RR	2 Indep.Coy.RR	
11 ST Pl.	12 ST Pl.	
No. 1 Sec.RhMP	No. 2 Sec.RhMP	
10 RR (Gwelo)		
1 CCP (Medical Corps)	2 CCP	
1 LAD (ASC)	2 LAD	

CCP was an abbreviation for Casualty Collection Post and LAD for Light Aid Detachment mainly used to augment repair facilities for vehicles and armament.

Directly under Divisional HQ came 1st Field Regiment (Artillery), C Sqn. SAS, a Company of RAR (detached from 1 RAR and based at Inkomo near Salisbury), the Rhodesian Defence Regiment and Training Depot at Cranborne Barracks, Salisbury, a Combat Tracker Unit (in Kariba), the Army Detention Barracks and all Administration Services and Training Establishments.

Administration Services included Engineering Workshops, Signals Workshops, Transport Workshops, Armoury Workshops, Medical Services, Ordinance Supply Depots, Pay Corps sub-units, Education Corps facilities and schools, legal services and catering and welfare organizations. This group was known as the tail of the Army and compared with other armies was very small. At that time and throughout the war it was very understaffed.

The Training Establishments consisted of a School of Signals (in Bulawayo), School of Infantry, Depot RR (Llewellin Barracks), Supply and Transport School (Llewellin Barracks) and the School of Military Engineering (SME), Bulawayo (Brady Barracks).

Training of their own recruits was carried out by RAR, RLI, Rhodesian Artillery and C Sqn. SAS. There were also courses run by Combat Tracker Unit in Kariba.

Other Corps and units were added and existing units expanded as the size of the Army grew post 1973.

We finished the morning off with voice procedure. We covered formal messages, degrees of precedence and classifications. We were told that formal messages had as precedence routine, priority, immediate and flash in order of increasing urgency.

Lieutenant McDermott told us about a junior officer who had requested extra ration packs and had sent the message out flash. He had got into a great deal of trouble. We wondered if this officer had been Lieutenant McDermott.

We were also told that messages were classified as restricted, confidential, secret, top secret and burn before reading!

The afternoon was spent revising fire control orders.

For the first time that evening we had guard duty and I was part of the guard. This was to become one the banes of our existence. We couldn't do the guard mounting because we had not yet covered it in drill, but since we had now fired the FN we were considered capable of doing guard duty.

A guard consisted of five men, a Guard Commander, a 2IC and three others. The guard commander and 2IC stayed in the guard room and woke the relief guard up when appropriate. The others took turns, two hours on, four hours off to patrol the camp particularly the armoury.

During winter in the Midlands it could be horribly cold. Pete Addison remembers that we had at our disposal a very hairy greatcoat to keep us warm and save our extremities from freezing. He spent some of his time watching rabbits, but never discovered their burrow.

Guard was basically from sunset to sunrise. The Guard Commander had to ring the Ops Room at 0530hrs to wake the duty Sergeant.

Tuesday 8 May

We were very tired after the night's guard duty and drill was terrible. We covered the high port from the order.

On the way to the lecture room we were again caught by the RSM and given a roasting. Beefy Barlow was particularly unimpressed, expressing the desire to "drift that RSM". Beefy, as an Old Miltonians prop, would have been quite capable of "drifting" anyone, but it might not have been a good Army career move!

Our morning lecture was on the main coding system of the Rhodesian Army, the slidex and plackard codes. This was very interesting and we practised coding and decoding messages until we were really quite good at it.

We then had a de-brief on Progress Test 1. We went over all the questions and were told that most of us were too verbose when often a one-word answer was all that was required.

The afternoon was spent learning how to strip, clean and reassemble the MAG as well as putting rounds in the belts.

The day finished with a rugby practice and a relatively early bed.

Wednesday 9 May

We went twice over the assault course before breakfast and were told about the Battle March for which we would soon start practising. This was a march, supposed to be done at the double, in full battle dress, incorporating the assault course and terminating in the firing of weapons on the range.

After a very brief and uneventful inspection - Sergeant Nel was even less of a stickler for spit and polish than Colour Wales - we had drill, covering saluting with weapons and the grounding and taking up of arms. Voice procedure followed, with a lecture given by Lieutenant McDermott on the various types of radio waves and the two basic types of radio in use. These, at that time, were the short range, direct line radios and the short wave radios that bounced the signal off the ionosphere and hence allowed reception over thousands of miles.

For the first time some of us knew a little bit more than our lecturer, but Lieutenant McDermott had done his homework and was able to field most of the "curve-ball" questions from the physicists amongst us.

We were shown the two most used operational radios, the A60, which we had already seen, and the A63. We then had a practical using the A60, actually transmitting messages. Both these radios were light and very sturdy. They operated off any one of ten fixed frequencies, no tuning was necessary. They could be used for ground to ground and ground to air communication. We were told that later in the course, we would do a practical exercise on ground to air liaison in conjunction with the Air Force.

The afternoon saw us on an eight-mile route march in weapon training order, down the Bulawayo-Gwelo road. We spent the evening working on a backlog of assignments, for me, a lecture on Idi Amin, the Geography project and studying for the second progress test due on Saturday.

Thursday 10 May

Things began well enough with a leisurely 0815hrs start and no inspection. The whole day was spent out in the field doing practical map-reading exercises. It made a welcome change being out in the bush and on our own for considerable periods, well away from the strict supervision of our instructors.

First, we took bearings, worked out back bearings and did resections and intersections. We then went on several short compass marches, moving from feature to feature and then through thick flat featureless bush on fixed bearings. We were being trained to have complete faith in our compasses and the very reliable 1:50 000 scale Rhodesian maps. The latter were used throughout the war and were as good as any maps that I have seen, before or since.

Talking to Lieutenant McDermott during the course of the day, we learned that we would spend some time at The School of Engineering at Brady Barracks in Bulawayo. We also learned that after leaving Gwelo most of us would only be going to Kariba for thirteen weeks before moving to new barracks that were being built in Inyanga village. Apparently the authorities saw the Eastern Highlands as the next "trouble spot".

As it turned out, after our 19 weeks training the intake, having become 3 Independent Company, was sent straight to Inyanga, where they had to camp for several weeks before the barracks were ready.

It was a very physical day, rounded off with a rigorous rugby practice.

We managed to snatch a half hour in the mess after dinner but had to get down to a bit of work with "lecturettes" due to be given next day and the progress test looming up. We fell into bed at 2300hrs.

Friday 11 May

We got up at 0430hrs. Although we sometimes didn't have inspections, we were seldom told in advance, so had to be prepared for one.

We went for a road run, followed by an ice cold swim in the small pool and then, after breakfast, it was service writing, with an emphasis on appreciations. Essentially, an appreciation was a reasoned sequence of thought leading to the best solution of a problem. We were to spend a great deal of time on this, as most planning of any sort in the Army, from organising a simple patrol to mounting a full-scale attack on a terrorist camp, required an appreciation of the situation. At our level we were to be taught the full appreciation and the battle appreciation.

The full appreciation was to be made with the following

sequence. Aim, factors, courses open (enemy and own), courses adopted and the plan. The most important factors affecting the appreciation were enemy strength and disposition, ground, and time and space. The battle appreciation was a drastically shortened version with the sequence aim, ground and plan.

Voice procedure followed, with a practical lesson on operating the TR28A. We had two sets between each squad of four and took turns tuning at different frequencies and transmitting messages. With dial tuning and the fact that we were transmitting in HF (high frequency) and indirectly, it was hard going, with reception at twos or even ones at times. However we persevered and made some progress.

After lunch we gave our "lecturettes". Topics included were the Watergate scandal, the EEC, American POWs in Vietnam, Northern Ireland and UDI. We had done our research and our presentations were interesting and detailed. We even got a compliment from our Course Officer, these being "like ducks' teeth" - scarce. It was an interesting afternoon.

We spent the evening scrubbing and polishing the barrack room in readiness for what we had been told was a major inspection the next day and swotting for our second progress test.

Saturday 12 May

This time the inspection was taken by WO2 Hallamore, the Cadet Wing Sergeant Major, amazingly with very little drama.

We then moved on to a lengthy debriefing on our military symbols exercise and then the equally lengthy second progress test. I felt that I had done much better this time.

Then it was off to Que Que for rugby. I played on the wing for the seconds and managed to run in a couple of tries off well timed feeds from Bryan McDermott (Christian names on the rugby field).

Playing at Fly Half for the opposition was Kevin Lamprecht from Barclays Bank, Kariba. In the bar after the game Kevin told me that he had been transferred. He then gave me the bad news that Chris Peters, the fellow who had replaced me in Internal Affairs (Intaf), had been killed while riding his motorbike late one evening. Kevin also told me that he had not been found until about an hour after the accident. I had never met Chris, but had heard that he was a good bloke.

I also had a long conversation with Lieutenant Colonel Davidson, School of Infantry Commandant. He came up to me and asked if I was Sanderson and was I on a regular officer's course at one stage. I wondered how the hell he knew that and then I realised that I must have mentioned it in the essay on "My Early Life", which he must have read. Good to see that he was taking an interest in us.

He asked me what I did in "civvy street" and I told him that I had been teaching Mathematics for four years. This surprised him and he asked how old I was. I told him 25 and that I had always looked younger than I was. I also told him that he was correct and that I had been there six years before on the same course as Johnny Dawson, Ian Maclean, Lyn Conbrink, Ron Marillier, Bruce Snelgar and Vince Boswell, all Captains now, but that I had left it after first phase of my own accord to go back to university. He asked me if I had any regrets and I told him none.

Some of us, including myself, were on guard with people standing in for us, so we couldn't linger long. Somebody gave us a lift back to School of Infantry.

Sunday 13 May

We had a lazy day most of Sunday. I caught up on a bit of work, namely finishing my Geography assignment, and then wrote a few letters.

We worked in Moyale. In this lecture room were photographs of all the officers' courses that had preceded us, regular and national service. It was amazing how many of the men in the photographs I knew. Rhodesia was indeed a small world at that time.

The list was quite long. I recognized Graham Vaughan (Intake 81, finishing September 1966), P. Fynn (82, October 1966), "Droopy" Drummond (83 December 1966), Billy Gordon (84, January 1967), Stewart McLeod and Hamish Copeland (85, March 1967), Pete Chalmers and Blaise Reynolds (86, May 1967), Charles Jupp (87, June 1967), Stan Lewin (89,

September 1967), Andre Maztak (93, April 1968), Gerry Alford (96, September 1968), Howard Reid (98, December 1968), Cillier Whitley (101, May 1969), Ian "Snorts" Northcroft (111, October 1970), Andy Gilbert (112, December 1970), John McCarthy and Mike Christianson (113, January 1971), Brian Varndell (124, August 1972) and Richard Way (125, October 1972). I also recognized some of the Course Officers and Instructors from my earlier time at School of Infantry, namely Major David Parker (later to be CO of the RLI, respectfully nicknamed "The King"), Captain John McVey and Sergeant Basil Lentner.

We got to bed our earliest yet, cheered by the fact that there were only two weeks to go before the end of first phase and, hopefully, a 48 hour pass.

Monday 14 May

Breakfast at 0630hrs, and the day began with a short inspection from Colour Wales (back from Salisbury), one hour of drill before a short interruption for an uneventful muster parade and two hours more drill. We covered compliments with weapons, the present from the shoulder, fix and unfix bayonets, port arms, cocking weapons and easing springs for arms inspections.

The unfix bayonets procedure caused a great deal of suppressed amusement when our instructor demonstrated it. In order to unfix bayonets it is necessary to place the rifle between the legs and crouch over it in a strangely suggestive position. We kept relatively straight faces, however, as we knew we would shortly have to follow suit.

Our arms were aching at the end of this lengthy drill session. Chucking a 9 pound rifle around for three hours was as good as a strenuous gym workout.

We moved to Moyale to do a practice written exercise on the full appreciation. This took us through to lunch. At the end of the exercise we were given another full appreciation to do by Tuesday 22 May.

After lunch we drew MAGs, one machine gun plus one belt of 50 drill rounds between two, and spent the next one and a half hours on basic operation, taking turns. The lesson was conducted as a drill.

On the command "Belt of 50 rounds, load!" we would adopt the prone position, grasping the small of the butt with the left hand and the trigger unit with the right. We would then check that the safety catch was in the "Fire" position, open the feed tray cover, place the end of the belt on the feed tray and close the cover.

Next came the command "Ready". This meant that we would set the sights to 300m (battle sights) and cock the gun with the right hand. The weapon was now ready to fire. The command for this was "Go ahead".

After firing, with rounds still in the belt, came the command "Make safe". At this we would open the feed tray cover, remove the belt, cock the gun, check the breech to make sure that it was clear of rounds, ease the parts forward, replace the belt, close the feed tray cover and put the sights down. We returned the weapons and finished the day with a revision session on Map Reading in preparation for the day compass march on Thursday.

For me the day had been hard going as I was an aching mass of muscle, having been knocked about a bit on Saturday. I had a swollen left knee and a sore left elbow. It had been hell lying down in the prone position during weapon training even though after our initial experiences we had displayed the presence of mind to wear camouflage jackets with the thin padding on the elbows.

308 days left and counting. The exact period of our National Service was 341 days, just short of a calendar year.

Tuesday 15 May

Drill was even more strenuous than it had been the previous day. This time we had four hours covering guard mounting procedure, port arms from the shoulder and drilling a squad. For the latter exercise we all took turns drilling the rest of the squad for periods of about ten minutes each.

This proved a lot more difficult than we expected as each of us quickly ran out of ideas. Colour Wales was his usual eloquent self. "The way you drill a squad, you gobshites will be flat out making Corporal, let alone getting commissioned!"

We doubled to the armoury to return our weapons and were waiting to hand them in when the RSM walked past. Pete Addison, who had been held up, was caught outside the armoury enclosure.

He must have slightly panicked and forgotten all we had learnt about paying compliments with a weapon and the fact that it was an RSM approaching him, not an officer. With his weapon at the shoulder, for some reason in his right hand, he chucked up a salute to the RSM with his left and uttered a very smart "Good morning sir!"

RSM Collyer went apoplectic. He couldn't believe what he had just seen.

"You stupid bastard! I haven't got bird shit all over my fucking shoulders, so you don't salute me! Also, have you not been shown how to do compliments with a weapon? You hold the rifle in your left hand! Your left hand! Do you understand?"

The RSM was so shocked that Pete got off with another very smart, "Yes sir!" The RSM stormed off, shaking his head.

The morning's lectures were on the organization of 1 Battalion Rhodesian African Rifles (RAR), as mentioned, the only regular African infantry regiment and 1 Battalion Rhodesian Light Infantry (RLI), the only regular European infantry regiment. During the course of the war the RAR expanded to three battalions but at that stage it consisted of just the one.

1 Battalion RAR was organized as follows:

Battalion HQ consisted of 5 officers and 23 men (5+23).

There were five infantry companies A,B,C,D and E (5+118 each).

Each company had 3 platoons (1+34).

There was an HQ Company (6+205) consisting of signals, mortar, motor transport, administration, medical, band, tracker and training platoons.

At that time the RAR was officered by Europeans. All personnel, other than a few attached European NCOs, were African. There were 36 officers and approximately 820 other ranks. Battalion HQ was in overall charge.

The HQ Company was split up into small specialist platoons. The Mortar Platoon was split into three sections with two 81mm mortars each, the Motor Transport Platoon included drivers and mechanics and the Training Platoon was responsible for a six-month training course for squads of 40 men at a time, taken in at one-month intervals. There was no shortage of recruits, and a three-week selection course chose the 40 from 480 applicants.

Each Rifle Company was split into three platoons with a young Officer in charge of each. Each platoon was split into a section with a Corporal or Lance Corporal in charge of each.

The Commanding Officer of the Battalion was a Lieutenant Colonel, with a Major as 2IC and a Major in charge of each Company. The Battalion Adjutant was a Captain, as was the 2IC of each Company.

Lieutenant McDermott was quite a fund of information on the RAR, having been "badged" with them. When I asked him how many Ndebele (the more "warlike" tribe, an off-shoot of the Zulu) and how many Shona (their implacable enemy) were in the RAR, I was surprised to get the answer that nearly all were Shona. The enmity between the two tribes continues today in Zimbabwe.

One Battalion Rhodesian Light Infantry, as a Commando Battalion, was split into one Base Group and three Commandos instead of four Companies, as would be the case with an ordinary Battalion. The Base Group consisted of several specialist Troops (instead of Platoons) and a Support Group, itself being split into a Recce Troop and an 81mm Mortar Troop. Later Base Group became Support Commando. There were supposed to be 36 Officers and 572 men but at that time there was a chronic shortage of men and there were, in reality, only about 70 to 80 men in each Commando. It had become necessary to channel selected national servicemen into the RLI to boost their numbers.

The afternoon saw us continue our instruction on the MAG. Things went mostly without a hitch. We were working in pairs, one simulating firing and one loading and carrying. I was with Billy Green. We were being "time trialed" and each pair was competing with the others.

We beat the rest on a drill, but realised in our haste that we had put the belt of rounds in the wrong way round. Technically, we should have immediately lifted the feed tray cover and turned it around, but because we wanted to be first to complete the drill, we kept quiet about it, hoping that our instructor would not notice. Unfortunately "Eagle Eyes" Wales spotted this, so Billy and I wound up doubling to the top of the nearby kopje and back with the MAG!

We were told that there would be no inspection or drill next day as we were to have our pre-classification shoot with the FN. As a result, after a rugby practice, we had a little bit of time to ourselves and had a few drinks (soft) in the mess and a bit of a chat.

The senior course men were due to be given their appointments on Thursday, and there was a bit of speculation as to who out of our course would get commissioned. There were the optimists who felt that we were so good that we would all be officers and the pessimists who felt that we would be lucky to get any. The uneasy feeling that some of us were being targeted for a return to Llewellin was growing, and we again feared that some of us would not even finish their time at School of Infantry.

Wednesday 16 May

We had a nice leisurely 0615hrs start, first drawing rifles, and had two runs over the assault course in full battle dress with weapons, all this in preparation for the dreaded Battle March.

We returned our rifles, had breakfast and then drew them again for the pre-classification shoot.

On the range, none of us did very well. There was quite a bit of wind and our groupings were all over the place.

The afternoon was spent at Gwelo Sports Club ushering and selling cool drinks at the Penguins rugby match. Our course had been "volunteered" to help. I was on the drinks stand and didn't get to see any rugby.

During the afternoon I bumped into David de Pinho, a boy whom I had taught at Prince Edward when he was in Form 1 in 1969. He was now a very prominent senior at Que Que High School. I remembered him well and recalled how I and Ian Wilkinson, another teacher, had gone to see him box for St Joseph's, along with his friend Larry Pratt, at the Braeside boxing club. He was very good.

The up-side of the whole business was that we were able to have a few drinks at Gwelo Sports Club after the game. "DG" Harris (former pupil) and Al Anderson (former teacher) from Prince Edward had scrounged a pass from Llewellyn and had come up to watch the game. They were in the senior intake, Intake 129, and were also to be given their appointments on return to Bulawayo.

Thursday 17 May

This turned out to be the best day in the Army so far, with our first full-scale day compass march exercise, called "Famba Zvishoma", which was Shona for "Little Walk". We found out that all the exercises in the Army had been given names, often very aptly.

We were divided up into groups of three and dropped off in the bush next to the Gwelo to Que-Que road with one A60 and one TR28 radio, two prismatic compasses, one protractor and one map. We were in weapon training order, carrying rifles. The idea was to move from RV to RV from 0900hrs to 1500hrs, getting the grid reference of our next destination, in code, once we reached the previous RV.

Once again we were amazed at how easy it was to read the Rhodesian 1:50,000 maps. It was great to be entirely on our own without somebody "on our backs" all the time. It was also interesting to put our faith in our compasses during the parts of the march when we were out of sight of obvious landmarks.

We were given a packed lunch at our final RV on the top of a gomo where we met up with our instructors. It was then back to Gwelo where, after rugby practice, we broke the rules to celebrate or commiserate with the Senior Course in the mess over their appointments. It was all their fault, as they insisted on us having beers! They had six Second Lieutenants, not bad, since the average for an intake was three or four.

Once again we speculated as to how many of our intake would be commissioned. While I was chatting to Digby about this he came up with the alarming thought that people we knew probably expected us to be commissioned. They assumed that if we were on the Officers' Course we would automatically become officers.

Friday 18 May

It seemed almost too good to be true to have another leisurely start to the day with once again no inspection and no drill. We spent all morning, about four hours, doing MAG weapon training tests again and again. The procedures really were becoming automatic, loading, unloading, making safe and the numerous stoppage drills.

Then we were off to the range for the MAG introductory shoot. We fired a total of 150 rounds each, three belts of 50, one each at 100m, 200m and 400m. At some stage I had a "runaway gun". This occurs when for some reason the firing pin continues to strike after one takes one's finger off the trigger. The remedy is to twist the belt to stop the rounds entering the feed tray, but quite a few rounds are discharged before one can react. This made for an interesting shoot.

My overwhelming impression was of a really lethal weapon with enormous firepower and amazing accuracy. With my vivid imagination, I wondered what it would be like to be on the receiving end of ten rounds a second from a MAG!

We spent the evening cleaning and polishing for the final Course Officer's inspection next day. The following Saturday inspection would be carried out by the OC Cadet Wing, Major Pelham, when hopefully we would be good enough to obtain our end of first phase 48-hour pass. We would also have to "pass off the square" meaning that our drill would have to be good as well.

Saturday 19 May

We had worked quite hard for this morning's inspection, but the result was to say the least depressing. It was a very lengthy inspection and no stone was left unturned.

We went to drill with the Lieutenant's words ringing in our ears. It seemed that if we didn't jack ourselves up we would still be doubling in six weeks' time and would not pass out of first phase. Colour Wales seemed annoyed at all this and consequently we had a very strenuous three hours of arms drill.

The first part of the afternoon I spent playing fly half for Gutu! At the rugby practice on Thursday, they had called for three volunteers to play for Gutu, who were short of players for their game against Gwelo Sports Club. It seemed to me that not many people could claim to have played rugby for Gutu, certainly it would be another half page in the memoirs. We weren't very good and we got thundered 35-4, coarse rugby at its best.

We then got into civvies and jumped on an RL to go out to Thornhill to watch the School of Infantry Firsts play the Air Force before having a few snorts. We persuaded the RL driver to stop on the way home for a hamburger and chips, before falling contentedly into bed.

Sunday 20 May

We were rudely awakened by the Duty Sergeant at about 0530hrs to be told that our course was on guard duty for the day and night sessions, starting at 0600hrs. Apparently the African demonstration troops, who were supposed to be on guard, had been deployed elsewhere. This meant that five of us would have to do the day shift and five the night shift. We quickly drew lots to decide who would be on which shift. I was lucky enough to draw the day shift, which meant a lightning change into weapon training order and a quick trip to draw weapons from the armoury, conveniently opened for us, before guard mounting.

Guard duty had the one advantage that, when in the Guard Room, one could get on with a bit of study and I managed to finish off the appreciation that we had been given.

During the evening we got word of riots in Gwelo's African township and distant police sirens could be heard. We wondered if this had anything to do with the African troops being deployed.

At about midnight, Graham Birch woke us up to tell us that the Guard had to be doubled as an FN and twenty rounds of ammunition had been stolen from 10 RR in Gwelo. This meant that ten of us were on Guard until 0600hrs.

Monday 21 May

We stumbled exhausted to the assault course, which we negotiated twice before moving off to breakfast and then the dreaded musters.

The morning's lecture was our first tactical lecture. It was on verbal orders, given at level of Platoon Commander with the emphasis on classical war (conventional war). First we learned the theory, then followed a practical demonstration by Lieutenant McDermott. It was clear that he had done this before. Then there was time for some of us to give orders to the group based on an imaginary scenario, with varying degrees of success.

Generally, orders were to be given in a standard sequence with the five main headings situation, mission, execution, administration and logistics and command and signals. 'Situation' covered details such as the ground, enemy forces, friendly forces and attachments and detachments. 'Mission' was usually a one sentence statement of the task to be carried out. 'Execution' was the most detailed part of the orders covering specific tasks for each section or attachment, depending whether we were in defence, attack or withdrawal.

'Administration and logistics' covered topics as varied as ration, water and ammunition re-supply, handling of prisoners-of-war, tools and, in defence, positioning of latrines.

'Command and signals' dealt with topics such as position of headquarters, radio channels, netting, code words and nicknames.

We were all issued with the "Rhodesian Army Aide-Memoire for Platoon Commanders", a document that we all used extensively throughout the war.

We quickly squeezed in a revision drill session before another lecture, this time on the organization of an Independent Company. We had a particular interest in this as most of us were destined to spend the last seven months of our National Service with No. 3 Independent Company. It was structured along the lines of any infantry company but with six regular personnel, namely a Major/Captain, Captain/Lieutenant, WO2 and three sergeants. All other personnel were national servicemen including three Second Lieutenants, one in charge of each of the three platoons, three Sergeants as Platoon 2ICs and nine Corporals as section commanders.

Weaponry consisted of rifles, one MAG per section and white phosphorus and HE grenades. Heavier weaponry would have to be brought in from other units.

The day dealt a blow for five of us, one of them being me, when yet again we were put on guard duty.

Tuesday 22 May

One hour's drill, during which we rehearsed "passing off the square", was followed by another tactical lecture, this time on the principles of war. These principles were selection and maintenance of the aim, maintenance of morale, offensive action, security, surprise, concentration of force, economy of effort, flexibility, co-operation and administration. It was made clear that all Officer Cadets had to learn these by heart and apply them intelligently in the study of tactics at the School of Infantry.

We handed in our appreciation and then doubled down to another lecture room for a very interesting lecture from Captain Cooper, of Regimental Wing, on the role of 81mm mortars in support of infantry. He had been a terrifying RSM at the School of Infantry in 1967. I certainly preferred him as an officer.

The 81mm mortar, used by the support units in the RLI and RAR and mortar platoons in the RR, had a maximum range of 4575m and fired a 3.2kg missile. Technically it could fire up to twenty rounds per minute, but ammunition supply and danger of barrel heat pre-ignition meant that it was never fired at more than the intense rate of 10 rounds per minute. The Rhodesian Army employed HE, HE colour and smoke rounds.

Captain Cooper told us that the communist equivalent was the 82mm mortar, which meant that they could use our mortar bombs but we could not use theirs.

After lunch we covered the duties of a night sentry (as if we hadn't had enough experience of this on guard duty) and revised drills on the MAG.

In anticipation of long nights of polishing ahead before our final first phase inspection, we managed a few drinks in the mess, followed by an early night. Daily inspections were perfunctory of late and so we took a chance – we were getting a little better at "cuffing it"!

Wednesday 23 May

Today's inspection was anything but perfunctory and once again we experienced the rough edge of Colour Wales' tongue. We again spent an hour rehearsing "passing off the square", where we were told that we were drilling like pregnant drum-majorettes.

We then went to draw weapons for our classification shoot. This turned out to be a total disaster. The wind was up and only Graham Birch classified. Our drill instructor made the rather obvious comment that this was definitely not our day!

The afternoon was spent practising the Battle March: five miles in squads of four, in full battle dress including steel helmet, carrying 30lbs of equipment each and sharing three FNs, with slings attached but carried at the port the whole way and a MAG with sling. For the Battle March proper one team of five from our course would be selected.

Half way through we had to negotiate the assault course with weapons slung around our necks and at the finish, at the range, we fired twenty rounds from the FNs and a full belt (50 rounds) from the MAG. Points were awarded for such niceties as keeping in step, not falling off obstacles on the assault course and the shooting.

After supper we went on a night compass march exercise named "Beacon Blunder", during which most of us got hopelessly lost and only made the rendezvous at close to midnight. Only Digby's section seemed to navigate correctly. That, combined with the fact that they managed to jump on a passing army truck, enabled them to reach the final rendezvous point earlier. Unfortunately Colour Wales, for some reason lurking in the bushes on the approach route, overheard Digby and Billy discussing their nefarious activity and asked them about it. Digby, in his own words vouchsafed recently, already labelled by Colour Wales as the "barrack room lawyer", suggested that they had used initiative. In view of the fact that the Army valued initiative, they got away with it.

On arrival back at School of Infantry we polished and cleaned until 0130hrs before dropping half dead into bed. Colour Wales was right, it hadn't been our day!

Thursday 24 May

We did not have an inspection at all. Obviously our instructor "had our number" and we went straight onto the Drill Square for two hours of practice. We did a little better.

We then moved on to draw weapons for our pre-classification MAG shoot. This time there was no wind and things went really well. All of us would have qualified had it been the classification shoot.

The afternoon was spent working on the two-inch mortar. It was explained to us that we would not fire the two-inch mortar but its replacement weapon, the 60mm mortar, later on in the course and therefore a certain amount of familiarity with the mortar was necessary. We learnt how to clean it, to firmly dig the base plate in before firing and how to range it and fire it.

After dark we were off again, this time on a night shoot with the FN. We fired with and without illuminants and were introduced to the Icarus flare for the first time. This consisted of a small rocket in a tube which fired the flare to a height of about 250 feet before it illuminated and floated down on a parachute. We were amazed at the amount of light that it threw out.

It had been another long day. We wondered if all the night activity during the last week of first phase was deliberately arranged to put us under pressure.

Friday 25 May

Two hours of drill left us with the feeling that we might after all be allowed to pass off the square, meaning that, as well as being granted leave, we would not have to drill again.

With the war hotting up, there being more and more infiltration and more and more contacts initiated, it was considered that drill took time away from more vital training and there was little, if any, during second and third phase. Colour Wales wanted to be sure, so he cancelled our two-inch mortar training and scheduled two extra hours of drill for the early afternoon.

The rest of the morning was spent watching African

demonstration troops doing section battle drills in the training area. I was hugely impressed with their weapon handling, their field-craft and their voice procedure. They were all seconded from the Rhodesia African Rifles and had obviously been very well trained, some with combat experience. So far we had had no training in this area and so they appeared doubly competent. They certainly gave us a high standard to aim for.

After lunch we did our extra drill and then lined up for pay parade to collect our wages of $19.21. On the way back to our barrack-room we were accosted by the RSM and inevitably copped another "rev" just to save him getting bored.

My batman, Honesty, had left a parcel on my bed from "Les Girls" in the Prince Edward School office. This contained all sorts of edible goodies which helped us through the long night of polishing and cleaning.

At about eight Wales dropped in from the Sergeants' Mess to see how we were going and to offer us advice. He left us saying "I reckon you'll get through all right, but you buggers better get me arseholes for this!" He was in a happier mood than we were as he had a few "shumbas" (Lion beers) under his belt no doubt.

As well as getting ready for the inspection, we had to study for Progress Test 3, to be written after the OC's inspection and passing off the square and before we would be given our pass. It was interesting to note that we had as yet not got the results of our second progress test. We were all really feeling the pressure and were dog-tired. Our eyes were standing out on stalks.

Saturday 26 May

We were ready for the OC's inspection at 0815hrs, standing by our beds with Colour Sergeant Wales and Lieutenant McDermott looking very smart in greens, the full dress uniform of the regulars. We waited and waited until about 0900hrs. There was no sign of Major Pelham.

Eventually Lieutenant McDermott went to Cadet Wing and returned with the news that we would be doing our progress test first. No word of explanation for the non-appearance of Major Pelham was offered.

We went up to Moyale and wrote our progress test, the hardest yet. We had all performed dismally. We then went back to the barrack-room and once again stood by our beds.

Shortly afterwards Lieutenant McDermott arrived with Major Pelham. We certainly were red-eyed from lack of sleep, but not as red-eyed as Major Pelham. He was also very smartly turned out in greens, but he was undoubtedly very much under the weather and his uniform contrasted strangely with his very white face. The less kind amongst us surmised that he had been on a bit of a bender the night before and had overslept. The more charitable felt that he was displaying severe cold symptoms!

We all snapped smartly to attention as he approached and I trotted out the by now time-worn "44440 Officer Cadet Sanderson I.M. sir!", but Major Pelham's heart was definitely not in it and the inspection passed without a hitch.

We moved onto the Drill Square, where we did not fare so well. We made a bit of a mess of things and at the end waited anxiously for Major Pelham's verdict. He told us that we would have to do some more drill during second phase to get up to scratch, but that we would still get our pass. We breathed a sigh of relief and were dismissed by Colour Wales.

So we were temporarily free at last, until 2359hrs on Monday. After our first legitimate beer in the mess, John Richardson and I climbed into his brother's car to travel to Bulawayo. I would then go on by plane to Salisbury.

We got to Bulawayo at about four and spent some time at the Terrace, a courtyard attached to the Selborne Hotel, drinking Castles and eating salt and vinegar crisps until it was time to catch my flight. I was dropped off at Coleen Stirling's place and was driven to the airport by her. I fell asleep as the plane took off and woke up as it touched down. My parents kindly picked me up at the terminal in town and took me to their place in Borrowdale to spend my leave. I collapsed into a very welcome bed.

Sunday 27 May

I awoke at 9am and lay luxuriating in the fact that I still did not have to get up unless I wanted to. What a great feeling. I took the dog for a long run in the huge area of bush nearby, had a leisurely afternoon and then went into Prince Edward School for the evening service.

Outside the Chapel I met Bill Cock, Housemaster of Selous House, where I had been a resident master. Bill was a large and very charismatic character, one of the warmest people I ever knew, and had been at Prince Edward since 1951. He was also the only Selous Housemaster that used to drive to Chapel (about 150m from Selous House). I remember Peter Kolbe making a joke about this some years later when he was guest speaker at the Old Boys annual dinner. Later, in the bar, Bill explained that he only drove to Chapel because it was Henry's night off (Henry was his cook) and he liked to drive on after the service to have the smorgasbord at Meikles Hotel!

I also met many of the boys I had taught the previous year.

Among the Selous House boys I chatted to were David Barclay, Peter Garnett, Doug Muir and Stephen Ziegler, all of whom were tragically killed in action within the next few years. David was with the RLI and died in action on 7 July 1977. Peter was a Lance Corporal, also in the RLI, and was killed in action on 4 October 1977. Doug with 3 Commando RLI died in action on 12 May 1979 and Stephen, a Lance Corporal, was killed in action in January 1978.

All deaths during the war were tragic but these were particularly hard to take, having seen them grow up before my eyes, from twelve-year-old boys to young men. For their families it must have been devastating.

Regrettably, Bill Cock is also no longer with us, having been murdered in a home invasion in Johannesburg in 1997.

I remember them all, and others, especially on Remembrance Day on 11 November in the UK, or at the dawn service on ANZAC Day on 25 April each year in Australia. When the "Last Post" and Elgar's "Nimrod" are played, it is particularly poignant. I know I am not alone to have these feelings, which intensify with age.

After the service I was invited to dinner at the bachelor's mess and then dropped into the Prince Edward School Hospital to chat with the nurses. I realised how much I missed being a schoolmaster and had a feeling that I would soon be back in harness, at Prince Edward School. Fortunately, for me, this did happen.

Monday 28 May

I spent the morning in town doing a bit of shopping and buying some clothes. From second phase onwards we would be allowed to wear civvies to supper and when off duty. The afternoon was spent quietly before it became time for the trip back to Gwelo. I was taking my Mazda bakkie. Before leaving, I dropped in to see my uncle and aunt, Alan and Edith Byrom, visited the Jameson house pub at Prince Edward and saw Peter and Glen Kolbe in Jameson House for a few beers.

I got to Gwelo at about 11.15pm and climbed into my bed in the barrack-room, not all that happy to be back. Civvy street had spoiled me!

Tuesday 29 May

Just to get us back on track, we started the day at 0615hrs with PT, three times over the assault course. At least there was no inspection. Our barrack room had to be neat and tidy, but the full kit layout was no longer required. After breakfast we moved onto our first lectures on the advance in classical warfare.

An advance could be carried out, in classical warfare, usually at battalion level or higher, for three main reasons: approaching to contact, following a deliberate enemy withdrawal or in pursuit. The principles of the advance were wide reconnaissance, maintaining momentum, use of air power, concentration of forces, flexibility and sound order of march. The advance was composed of an advance guard, a main force, mobile troops and flank guards.

We then proceeded to look at the advance at section level in the form of section battle drills. These were to form a huge part of our training over the next few weeks, as there was so much to them.

The first section battle drill covered battle preparations. These included personal camouflage, weapons serviceable, radios functional and netted and Section Commander's orders.

The second section battle drill covered reaction to effective enemy fire. Most men would instinctively drop to the ground when under effective enemy fire. This action would generally be wrong because the enemy would usually open fire when his target was in a place offering little or no cover. The best course would be to run and weave towards effective cover, making a difficult target. This action would lead to loss of control by the section commander unless carried out as a drill.

First would come the executive order from the Section Commander as "Take cover". Then each man would run to the nearest cover, preferably not more than 20 metres away. Every man would then dive into his cover and crawl so that the enemy could not have his sights on him when he reappeared. Any man who actually spotted the enemy would return the fire. This drill could be summarized as follows: take cover, dash, down, crawl, observe, sights, fire.

The third section battle drill covered location of the enemy. This was not easy. There were three stages to this drill. The first was observation – looking in the area from which the thump came and searching for movement, smoke or anything unusual. The second was fire – the Section Commander directing Riflemen to fire two shots at a time into likely cover. The third was movement – the entire section moving towards the enemy to draw fire.

The fourth section battle drill dealt with offensive action. Once the enemy position was known, offensive action would be taken. This usually consisted of fire and movement to gain a favourable position for the final assault. Fire and movement meant that half the section would move forward while the other half provided covering fire. We would practise this ad infinitum.

The fifth section battle drill covered the assault. This involved, among other things, a machine gun position and other groups giving cover to the assaulting troops.

The sixth was reorganisation. This included a sweep of the area looking for hiding enemy and a repeat of battle preparations.

The fourth and fifth drills gave us the most trouble during our training. Much would depend on the ground, which was different with every drill.

The last hour of the morning's lectures was spent on section formations and field signals. Formations consisted of single file, double file, arrowhead, spearhead, extended line and diamond.

Field signals were taught for silent communication in the field. In the main these were given using arm or hand movement. For instance, the signal to go back was to whirl the hand round above the head, while halt was the stop signal as used when driving. Two fingers placed on the shoulder indicated the Platoon Commander and two fingers on the arm the Section Commander.

The signal for "close in to me at the double" gave us a certain amount of amusement: one hand on the head with the other one fist clenched moving up and down.

The afternoon was spent doing mortar training tests and watching a film on the use of fire. We finished relatively early and were told that we would spend the last part of the afternoon moving to a new barrack room, Montgomery, closer to the mess. This took us about an hour.

The evening was spent in the mess enjoying being in civvies and, quite legally now, having a few beers. It was also great to know that there would be no inspection and that the day would start at 0815hrs.

Wednesday 30 May

The morning was spent on the MAG classification shoot. This time I classified as a marksman without any trouble at all, as did most of the course. No runaway gun this time.

The afternoon was spent doing another Battle March practice. Our fastest team was four minutes short of the record.

Someone on the course had heard, I think from a senior intake, that after first phase we could get the odd evening pass. At the end of the day we asked for one, but it was no go. This left us a bit disgruntled. After all, we had done well in the MAG classification shoot and had come close to the Battle March record.

We all stayed behind at the bar after dinner to have a few beers and for the first time morale was a little low. Statements like "What the hell do we have to do in this Army to be treated like men?" and "I'm sick of this bloody Army!" abounded. Perhaps our brief taste of civilian life over the weekend had made us less military.

I remember one "voice of reason" in the form of Charlie Lenegan suggesting that maybe we were expecting too much in the way of privileges now that we were in second phase and that since we could not do much about things, we may as well accept the privileges we were given and be content. We calmed down a bit – things can seem better after a couple of drinks – and had a fairly early night.

Thursday 31 May

During the first lecture of the morning it became obvious why we had not been given the pass the previous evening. It all hinged on the results of our progress tests. For the second test, they were not too bad but, for the third test, even we could see they were far from impressive.

Results of tests were generally handed out to us on a piece of paper with the column headings "Name", "Percentage", "Pass/Fail" and "Remarks". A pass mark was 60%. Regulations stated that if one got over 70% one was supposed to get a "Good" under remarks, over 60% a "Fair", over 50% a "Weak" and if under 50% a "Very Weak".

With Progress Test 2 we got one "Good", seven "Fairs" and four "Weaks". Progress Test 3 was markedly different. We were given two "Fairs", six "Very Weaks" and, no doubt as a result of complete frustration on the part of Lieutenant McDermott, who threw SD protocol to the wind, four "Pathetics". Only two of us had passed. Our highest mark had been 68.5% and our lowest 18%. It had been a complete disaster.

As a result, a seriously irritated Lieutenant McDermott informed us that only the two who had passed would be given weekend leave, and that even they were lucky.

For some of us the cancellation of passes was not too desperate, as we would have to play rugby on Sunday afternoon, but we might have been able to do something on Saturday!

After the tests de-briefing we moved onto a lecture on the organization and roles of a TF (Territorial Force) battalion. There were active TF battalions and reserve TF battalions. The active TF battalion was organized very much along the lines of the RAR battalions, but with all command positions taken by territorials. There were some attached regular personnel for training and administration purposes, usually three Majors, a Captain and sundry NCOs.

The CO was a territorial Lieutenant Colonel, the OCs of the five companies – A, B, C, D and HQ – were territorial Majors and Company 2ICs were territorial Captains. Each of the platoons in HQ Company, the signals, administration, MT and mortar platoons and each of the three infantry platoons in A, B, C and D companies had territorial Lieutenants or Second Lieutenants in charge. On paper the total strength was 30 officers and 620 men.

The establishment of the reserve battalions was much the same, except they did not have a mortar platoon.

The active battalions were 1RR (Rhodesia Regiment) based in Salisbury and 2RR based in Bulawayo. The reserve battalions were 5RR and 8RR based in Salisbury and 6RR and 9RR based in Bulawayo.

There were composite battalions, organized along the lines of a reserve battalion, with a mixture of reserve and active personnel, in Gwelo (10RR) and Umtali (4RR). Active personnel had a greater call-up commitment than reserve personnel.

The more mathematical amongst us asked what had happened to 3RR and 7RR. Apparently these had once existed during the period of the Federation of Rhodesia and Nyasaland (1953 to 1963) when they were still designated as 3RRR and 7RRR (Royal Rhodesia Regiment). 3RRR was an active battalion and 7RRR was a reserve battalion in Northern Rhodesia (now Zambia).

As recruits, regardless of where we would be posted when leaving School of Infantry, we currently wore the Rhodesia Regiment beret badge. I had noticed that the Maltese cross on the badge closely resembled the one that appeared on the badge of the King's Royal Rifles (the 60th), a British regiment, and wondered if there was some connection. The 60th were a rifle regiment and we were referred to as Riflemen rather than Privates, as were they. Subsequent research has revealed that as a result of the affiliation between the Rhodesia Regiment and the King's Royal Rifles during the First World War, RR did indeed model the badge on that of the 60th and adopted the rank of Rifleman.

The rest of the morning was spent on an introduction to

the SMC (sub-machine carbine). It looked like a toy, but working on the blow-back principle it was effective, firing small bursts up to 200m. We learnt to strip and clean it, the load and unload and the working of the firing mechanism.

Lunch was a sombre affair while we inevitably discussed the cancellation of our passes. The two who were offered the passes decided not to take them, in a show of support for the rest. Digby Neuhoff was particularly disappointed. He was the only married man on our course and had organized a weekend with his wife, Frankie, at the Midlands Hotel in Gwelo.

After lunch we had five-minute personal interviews with the Course Officer and Course Instructor. None of us came out of the interviews unscathed. I was told that they were pleased with my academic results but that I was altogether too quiet and too polite when giving orders. I assumed that they were referring to an incident the previous day at the range when I had been put in charge of getting the ammunition out of the RL for the shoot. I had used the word "please" when telling someone where to stack the ammo and had copped a "rev" for not giving orders properly. "You never say 'please' when giving orders! Just give them!"

They then asked me if I had any questions about the course. I asked Lieutenant McDermott if he would reconsider re-instating our weekend passes, as when we had written our last progress test we had been under a lot of pressure. I saw as soon as I said it that this was not a good idea. The reply was terse, to say the least. "No. First of all none of you really deserve it. Secondly, once your officer gives his decision you do not question it."

During these interviews, two of us were told that they were being sent back to Llewellin to complete their basic training there. It had been as we feared, and we felt even more demoralised.

It was interesting that we then moved onto bayonet fighting and could vent any spleen we had on unresisting sacks. I found myself wondering if the recent sequence of events had been more meticulously planned than we realised.

The day finished with a night compass march. We fared a little better this time than the last even though the ground was rougher and the legs of the march were longer. We were in bed by 2230hrs.

Friday 1 June

The two who were being "RTU'd" returned kit issued at School of Infantry. They at least got their weekend pass, only being required to report to Llewellin on Monday. We said our farewells and then went off to the training area for a practical on section battle drills.

We spent the morning tearing all over the countryside in every formation, giving all the field signals and doing all the drills, with many none-too-complimentary comments from our instructors. We did feel that we were better at the end than at the beginning.

For the first time we had used blank rounds. A blank firing attachment was screwed into the barrels of the FNs or MAG.

The afternoon session involved a lecture on grenades followed by a practical, in which we threw dummies. We covered characteristics of the M962 (Mills) and M67 grenades. The M962 had segmented casing for easier fragmentation, could only operate after screwing in a seven-second fuse, had an injury radius of 45 feet and a fatal radius of 15 feet.

The M67 had a fuse already in place with a four-second delay. Its casing was not segmented with fatal and injury radii the same as the Mills grenade.

At the end of the day we were told that we would be given a Saturday morning local pass. At least this was something.

In the evening we seriously drowned our sorrows in the mess. Some of Intake 129 from Llewellin came by and had a few drinks with us. They were on their way to their posting. With them was the former pupil of mine, "DG" Harris, who had been at Llewellin and whom I had bumped into at the Penguins rugby match. It was good to catch up with him.

Saturday 2 June

We all woke up this morning a little more cheerful after our night in the mess. We all went into town in civvies. I ducked into a barber-shop and was halfway through a haircut when in walked Rob Mutch and said "Hurry up. We're on guard duty in 20 minutes."

For the first time I thought about deserting! Of all the bloody luck, would you credit it? I had a definite sense of humour failure and uttered a few expletive-rich sentences, as did all those who suddenly found themselves on guard duty. So Saturday was wiped out. They were certainly getting their $1 a day out of us!

Sunday 3 June

Guard duty finished at 0600hrs. Some of us had done two lots of guard duty. We had a quiet morning putting together a few sketches for our initiation, to be held in the NS Officer Cadet Mess on Wednesday.

We had been told by our instructor and the new senior intake (Intake 130) that we had to perform a concert/variety show for them and all cadet wing staff. Apparently there were no holds barred, and we were allowed to take off anyone from the Commandant downwards with impunity. It was a chance to let off a bit of steam and again, we began to feel a little bit more cheerful. Digby was also a little bit happier, having seen his wife on Saturday morning (she decided to come down anyway) and also having spent Sunday morning with her at the School of Infantry pool.

In the afternoon we went to play rugby against Selukwe at Selukwe. Our team consisted of Lieutenant Colonel Davidson at centre, Major Shute as prop, ten members of Intake 131 and three others. Unbeatable, one would have said. We scored the first try and thought it was going to be an easy game, but the interception of a pass to me from Colonel Davidson gave Selukwe a try and we eventually went down narrowly.

We had a few drinks in the Selukwe Club before going into Gwelo and illegally dropping in to the local cinema. We saw "Harold and Maude", later to become a cult movie. It seemed to us, at the time, that Harold could have done with a bit of army discipline and I'm quite sure we totally missed the point of the film.

Monday 4 June

We arrived at the Drill Square for musters. There was only one other squad there, an African squad. Wales arrived and said "Let's fuck off", so we did.

Colour Wales wanted to get started on our scheduled compass march right away and didn't stand much for ceremony anyway. We didn't object.

Over the period of the course we got the feeling that Colour Wales was not exactly chums with RSM Collyer. Shadows from the past no doubt!

Unfortunately for us it was out of the frying pan into the

fire. Colour Wales gave us the glad tidings. The Cadet Wing Sergeant Major, Sergeant Major Hallamore, in the interests of discipline, had decided to have a musters for all Officer Cadets, national service and regular, outside Cadet Wing every morning Tuesday to Friday

The rest of the day was spent on our final compass march with weapons and radios, covering in all about 16 miles. Once again it was very pleasant to be on our own with nobody on our backs. All went smoothly.

Tuesday 5 June

We were right to dread the new daily musters. This consisted of forming up in squads on the lawn outside the Cadet Wing and being inspected by Sergeant Major Hallamore. On our first day we were threatened with extra drill because of alleged poor turn-out. Our belts in particular were supposedly "gungy".

First up was a lecture on the grouping system, basically how available forces could be feasibly divided up, from Captain Fawcett BCR (Bronze Cross Rhodesia) and Sword of Honour, School of Infantry 1966. He was a very energetic man and a very fine soldier. His nickname was "Chongwe", the Shona word for cockerel.

We then moved on to platoon battle drills with Lieutenant McDermott. There were four platoon battle drills, battle preparation, reaction to effective enemy fire, offensive action and reorganisation.

Location of the enemy was deemed to be taken care of at section level, as was the assault, considered to be part of offensive action. One point to make about platoon battle drills was that the platoon should not be committed to an attack before it was apparent that the section initially fired upon was unable to overcome the enemy opposition.

Formation, basically the positioning of the various sections, was important and hinged on whether the advance was along a road or across country.

The formation for the advance down a road was a point section in the lead, the Platoon Commander's group following, the Platoon Sergeant's party next and a left and a right rear section at the back. The formation for the advance across country was one up or two up. The one up formation started with a point section at the front and a left and a right rear section at the back, with the Platoon Commander's group and the Platoon Sergeant's party in between. The two up formation had a left and a right point section and a single rear section.

The afternoon was spent on the SMC, particularly training tests.

After rugby practice we had a few drinks in the mess and resolved not to let things upset us. We just had to accept that the Army was the Army and that a de facto first phase still existed to a certain extent. We then went back to the barrack room and polished our brasses to make them less gungy. We had to polish our stick boots as well as we were going to be given revision drill next day.

Wednesday 6 June

At musters we were the only squad and so had Sergeant Major Hallamore's full attention. Our brasses got through, but he noticed that we did not have backing for the flashes on our berets and told us to fix this up before next musters.

We went to the Drill Square and did revision of all the drill we had done in first phase. On the whole we seemed to remember it quite well.

The old humour had not deserted the Course Instructor. At some stage in the proceedings I made a mistake during a drill movement. Colour Wales did not mince words.

"Sanderson you awkward bastard, you still don't know how to drill. The only chance you have of getting commissioned is if your ears turn to arseholes and shit pips on your fucking shoulders!"

Lectures were on the organization and roles of artillery and types of fire. There was only one artillery regiment in the Rhodesian Army, the First Field Regiment. It consisted of thirty-two 25-pounder guns. The regiment was divided into four batteries (the artillery equivalent of a company) of eight guns each. Each battery was divided into two troops of four guns each.

Like the Rhodesia Regiment, the First Field Regiment was a territorial unit. The Regiment was commanded by a Lieutenant Colonel with a Major as 2IC, each battery a Major or Captain, each troop a Lieutenant or Second Lieutenant.

At the time and throughout the war, the CO of First Field Regiment was Lieutenant Colonel Robin Brown, a territorial. He had worked his way up from Gunner, the artillery equivalent of a Private. I spent the last five years of the war in artillery and got to know him well. He understood his men and really looked after them. I had enormous respect for him.

Each gun was in control of a Sergeant with a Bombardier, the artillery equivalent of a Corporal, as 2IC. All these were territorials. On paper each gun crew consisted of eight men. The RSM and the four Battery Sergeant Majors were also territorials.

There were several regular officers and NCOs to help with administration, training and with the light workshops troop who maintained the guns.

The types of shell used were HE and smoke. Delay fuse for air-burst were available but unreliable, and were seldom if ever used.

The guns could fire up to 13,400 yards on super charge but were seldom used for ranges more than 10,000 yards at the most on charge three, to avoid excessive barrel wear. One, two, three or four charges in bags were placed in a shell casing to propel the shell, which was loaded first, to fire the guns on charge one, two, three or super charge. Rates of fire were from very slow, at one round per minute, to intense, at 5 rounds per minute.

Fire support could be called in by giving the grid reference of the target and the target bearing from the observer. The gun position would send in the first shell and the observer could then zero the fire in by saying left, right, up or down so many yards. The fire from a 25-pounder was very accurate and troops could advance under the shell trajectory 300m behind the line of shell burst even on a predicted shoot, where fire is initially based on map reading only.

The rest of the morning was spent on an introduction to patrols. There were two types of patrol, reconnaissance or recce patrols and fighting patrols. The recce patrol was usually of minimum strength, carried out in order to gain information on enemy dispositions, to obtain topographical information and to locate obstacles, mines and wire.

The fighting patrol was of a size commensurate with the requirement at hand. It was organized to interfere with enemy patrols, to create diversions, to carry out raids and to take prisoners.

The minimum size of a recce patrol was one officer or NCO and four men. The minimum size of a fighting patrol was one officer and eight men. We were told that during the Korean War, US fighting patrols could be up to company strength.

We focused on patrols at platoon level. With patrols there was usually time to prepare thoroughly. The rough sequence leading up to a patrol was as follows.

First a warning order was received from the Company Commander and the patrol leader, usually the Platoon Commander or 2IC, would go to Company HQ and be briefed.

The patrol leader then made an appreciation and a plan, prepared orders, prepared a model of the ground to be covered, issued the orders, carried out any necessary rehearsals, briefed the rest of the defensive position on the timing of the patrol and the passwords for the returning patrol, organized the testing of arms and equipment, inspected the patrol, carried out the patrol and was debriefed by the Company Commander or IO. Patience and silent movement on patrols was essential.

The afternoon was spent doing the Battle March proper. Our team of Pete Addison, Digby Neuhoff, Rob Mutch, Charlie Lenegan and myself broke the record, which had stood since June 1971.

For two years other courses had tried and failed, including the regular courses. The old record was 373 points – the new one 376. We were rather pleased with ourselves. We had just enough time before supper to get small pieces of cardboard behind the flashes on our berets, ready for the next day's musters.

That evening we had our initiation in the mess. All the instructors and officers from all the courses plus most of the personnel from regimental and tactical wings were there. It was our turn to have a legitimate go at our tormentors, and we produced several skits pulling the Army and our instructors to bits.

The most popular skit consisted of a solo effort by Beefy Barlow. He delivered a stuttering and totally incompetent set of orders which were extremely funny. After this "Beefy's Orders" became an oft-requested party piece on social occasions, that and his fine rendition of "My Dingaling".

All of this was brilliantly received, the regulars laughing at all the jokes aimed at them more than the cadets in the senior course. Colour Wales in particular seemed really pleased with his course and everyone partied on until 0200hrs next day. A lot of what happened was a bit of a blur, but I remember that at some stage somebody from Intake 130 threw a primed thunderflash through the mess window. I and others took a few steps back and waited for it to go off. It could seriously damage fingers if held while it detonated, but otherwise it just made a very loud noise. However Charlie Lenegan quickly picked it up and threw it back out of the window. It detonated a second later. It had not been a bright move and this was volubly pointed out to him by one of the officers.

The party gradually got wilder and wilder. Intakes 131 and 130 had a bottle-throwing fight, with a considerable number of near misses. Fire extinguishers were involved at some stage. I know that Colour Wales was in the thick of it, an absolute maniac when in his cups!

Thursday 7 June

We all felt like death warmed up in the morning. Somehow we got through musters, helped by the fact that Sergeant Major Hallamore wasn't feeling all that great either.

We then moved onto a lecture on patrol orders. These had much the same headings as other types of orders, namely ground, situation, mission, execution, administration and logistics and command and signals.

These orders had to be given slowly and by stages, the members of the patrol being allowed to ask questions as the various points arose. The orders had to be detailed, they had to cater for all foreseeable contingencies and they had to be completely understood by every member.

During smoke break at 0900hrs Colour Wales arrived with the news that Staff Sergeant Bester and Sergeant Pretorius from the NS Cadets' Mess were having a sense of humour failure about the state the place was in after the previous night's revels. We were duly dispatched to the mess by Lieutenant McDermott and after a blast from Staff Sergeant Bester, we spent the next half hour cleaning dried fire extinguisher fluid off the ceilings and walls.

Then it was back to Moyale to get the second half of the lecture, this time on debriefing of patrols and writing patrol reports. After the patrol there would be a debriefing by a senior officer and a patrol report would have to be written out. Both these would cover destination of patrol, size and composition, task, time of departure and return, routes in and out, terrain, enemy, map corrections, condition of patrol, including any casualties, and any conclusions or recommendations.

To consolidate the lectures, we finished the morning with two films, "Dangerous Journey" and "Fighting Patrols".

The afternoon was spent with a demonstration on setting

up the trip flare, to be used mostly in defence or ambushes, and then the SMC introductory shoot on the 30-yard range. We fired the weapon lying, kneeling, from the shoulder and even from the hip like Audie Murphy!

We had a very quiet evening and were in bed by 2100hrs, our earliest night yet. For the first time I even did a bit of non-military reading before lights out. I had taken out a P.G. Wodehouse from the Camp Library.

Friday 8 June

The day began with a three-hour lecture on company battle procedure, in Ashanti, which involved bringing together a great deal of the tactics we had already learnt.

The aim of company battle procedure was to ensure that the private soldier went into battle at the right time and place knowing exactly what part he had to play.

There were four well-tried principles. Commanders at all levels had to anticipate future tasks, everyone had to have a thorough knowledge of the organization of the company, called the "grouping system", there had to be efficient drill for reconnaissance and the issuing of orders and there had to be concurrent activity at all levels within all groups.

The most important of these principles was the efficient drill for reconnaissance and the issuing of orders. Most essential was the initial time appreciation.

The Company Commander had to insure that sufficient time was allowed for junior commanders to carry out reconnaissance, planning and the issuing of orders. This was best done by working backwards from a known time and allocating time for each commander.

Lieutenant McDermott worked carefully through the principles, dealing, in this case, with the advance to attack, with the use of a cloth model. The cloth model was an ingenious set-up in which a large heavy cloth was placed over raised objects placed to create a contoured model of a landscape on which various tactics could be displayed. This could cover such things as ambush, defence, advance, attack and withdrawal.

Lieutenant McDermott went through the original positions and movement of the reconnaissance groups, the orders groups, various echelons, "F" Echelon (the fighting group), "A" Echelon (the immediate support group) and "B" Echelon (the rear support group). He went over the RV positions, forming up positions (FUPs) and assembly areas.

Essentially we were being given an overall picture. We were quite amazed at the amount of thought and preparation that had to go into a battle procedure. We couldn't help wondering what must have gone into planning and carrying out a battle at divisional level, such as the battle of El Alamein. It had been a thoroughly worthwhile morning.

The afternoon was spent converting to the sub machine gun (SMG) from the SMC and firing it on the 30-yard range, followed by a lecture on the use of the 28R anti-tank grenade and the 32Z anti-personnel grenade both fired from the barrel of the FN.

Things had proceeded fairly well over the last few days; we hadn't made any major faux pas and we were granted a pass from 1700hrs Friday to 2359hrs Monday. Monday was Whit Monday, hence the extra day. Pete Addison, Digby Neuhoff and I took off for Salisbury in my Mazda truck, our morale higher than it had been for some time.

I dropped Pete and Digby off at the Jameson Hotel, where they were being picked up, and drove to Borrowdale to spend the weekend with Mervyn Thompson, then teaching Latin at Prince Edward. He had kindly offered me a place to stay any time I was in Salisbury.

Saturday 9 June

After a leisurely start to the day Mervyn and I went to the Highlands Park Hotel for a long late lunch, mostly liquid, and then went off to a party in Mount Pleasant somewhere. I remember a lot of girls, something that after Kariba had been hugely missing in my life, a lot of fun and an awful lot of drink. Things wound up after the sun was up.

Sunday 10 June

This was definitely a day that I wanted to pass as quickly as possible. Mervyn and I were very much the worse for wear. We woke up late and mooched about the house all day with a few gentle beers in the evening before an early bed.

Monday 11 June

Another gentle day was called for and after having lunch and spending the afternoon with my parents, I picked Digby and Pete up from the Jameson Hotel for an uneventful trip back to Gwelo.

Tuesday 12 June

We were up early and put together kit for a two-day night patrol exercise in the field. Some we already had and some we drew from the QM Store. We were introduced for the first time to the renowned rat-pack (ration pack), something that would become familiar to all Rhodesian servicemen throughout the war. We then loaded up the RL before a bitterly cold journey to Gwenoro Dam with wind and heavy guti (a persistent drizzle).

We arrived at our base camp, were briefed on the recce patrol, which was to have the purpose of establishing exact enemy positions, and then given two hours to write up detailed orders and make up a model on the ground of the area to be patrolled. We were told that one of us would be chosen to give the orders.

When the time came it turned out to be me. I gave what I thought was a reasonable set of orders. Lieutenant McDermott was not impressed.

"Sanderson, that was appalling. You were cuffing it. Patrol orders must cater for all possible contingencies and you simply haven't done that. They must be given slowly and by stages. You just blurted the whole thing out and only paused and asked for questions twice! We'll give you another hour and then another one of you can give the orders and you will carry out tonight's patrol using these."

"Beefy" Barlow gave the next set of orders and copped a slightly less severe "rev" before we began preparations for the patrol.

We left at 1900hrs, crossing Gwenoro Dam in rubber boats and stumbling around the countryside, stopping every now and then to listen for the enemy, lying on the cold ground for up to 30 minutes with our teeth chattering until we moved on.

Eventually we heard talking and got as close as we could to the sound to try and gauge numbers. As far as we could see there were three of them, probably demonstration troops. Then it was back to the base, crossing the dam by boat again. I couldn't help thinking that it was all a bit like "playing soldiers", something I hadn't done since I was a young boy.

We sat round a fire – it was really cold by now – and were told what a mess we had made of things. Then it was bed under a bucksail. Fortunately we had had the presence of mind to bring sleeping bags.

Wednesday 13 June

We were up early and washed the camouflage cream off our faces. This stuff took a bit of getting off. We snatched a quick breakfast from our rat-packs and then prepared orders for a fighting/snatch patrol. We were to go out and capture one of the enemy.

This time Digby Neuhoff and Rob Mutch gave the orders and did a good job. Our instructors were less scathing of them. All this took most of the day, as we had to thoroughly prepare these orders and construct models on the ground to facilitate their delivery.

The same sort of things occurred on our patrol as the previous night. At one stage my section lay on the ground for one and a half hours, inducing a freezing spasm that I thought would never end despite the fact that I had on a jersey and a camouflage jacket.

Eventually the section that had secured the prisoner came back and we crossed the dam again. Halfway across we were fired on by some of the "enemy" and returned fire with the MAG, for which we later copped a "rev". Apparently this was unwise, as the flashes from our machine gun would give away our position on the water.

The section that secured the prisoner felt that the whole thing had been a little contrived. They weren't quite sure how to go about it and had just leapt out pointing weapons and grabbed the first person they could get their hands on. No resistance was offered. No doubt the "enemy" were as cold as we were and wanted the whole exercise to end.

After a short debriefing we finally got to sleep at 2400hrs.

Thursday 14 June

We were up at 0600hrs and washed, shaved and fed by 0700hrs. We struck camp and returned to School of Infantry to hand our equipment in. After lunch we met in Taungup, once again our lecture-room. The new intake, Intake 132, having arrived on Monday (no holiday for them), were using Moyale.

We had a quiz, one half of the course against the other on military aspects, with a crate of beers as the prize. It didn't matter which half won, the crate was shared.

The instructors then told us that we would get away from Army topics for a while. We had a game of "three minutes please", a game where one was given a word or phrase and had to put together a talk on it, speaking right away, for three minutes without a pause of more than five seconds. Topics were things such as "equilibrium", "a dark horse" and "night-soil".

Billy Green had to talk on "night-soil". With absolutely no idea as to what it was he launched into a monologue about how he happened to be an expert on it and, when analyzing it, spread it out on a glass plate to do microscope work on it. Colour Wales all the time was killing himself laughing. We wondered why, as Billy's talk didn't seem to be that funny. At the end we were told that "night-soil" was a euphemism for excretion that would be picked up every night in carts from houses in medieval times.

After rugby practice we had a night in the mess before turning in. Our hearts went out to the poor bastards in 132, furiously polishing and cleaning in their barrack-room. To add to their woes they, unlike us, had been issued with ankle puttees, obviously the shortage had been temporary.

Friday 15 June

We were up at 0600hrs and after a quick breakfast, it was onto the Selukwe-Gwenora Road for a practical on platoon battle drills, two men to each section, as our course was now down to 10. The other members of the platoon were imaginary.

There was a point section advancing down the middle of the road followed by the Platoon Commander's party, then the Platoon Sergeant's party followed by a left rear section and a right rear section in the bush to the left and right of the road, each about 50m apart.

We advanced, to be fired upon by the demonstration troops.

Whichever section was first fired upon, usually the point section, had to radio the Platoon Commander and explain the situation to him. He would then decide how to group the rest of his platoon to take the enemy position using fire and movement and skirmishing.

There was a lot of screaming and shouting by the DS (directing staff) with any mistakes being volubly drawn to our attention. We all took turns to be Platoon Commander or Platoon Sergeant and we walked miles and were very tired by the end.

We got back to our barrack-room to find that we had had an inspection by Sergeant Major Hallamore in our absence and as a result our weekend passes had been cancelled. Apparently we hadn't dusted the lampshades.

Hell, we were mad. Colour Wales wasn't very happy either. He felt, I suppose, that it was an insult to him as our Course Instructor and seeing our disappointment took it upon himself to let us take a pass anyway. I have often wondered if he got into trouble over this – I hope not.

I and five others were on the almost inevitable guard duty to wind up a pretty exhausting day.

Saturday 16 June

Guard duty finished at 0600hrs and I was off to Salisbury in John Richardson's car, in my case for a quieter weekend than the last one. I spent time once again with my folks.

My father and I decided to go and see the Italian rugby team playing Rhodesia at the Police Grounds. The Prince Edward School rugby team had been playing one of the curtain raisers and I walked past the Prince Edward boys' stand with my obviously military haircut to shouts of "Hello, sir" and "Rusty – the old soldier!" Most of them knew they would be following in my footsteps soon, but they enjoyed the spectacle nevertheless.

Sunday 17 June

I woke at a more sensible hour than normal and had a run before a leisurely breakfast. Then it was off to Nat Baker's for drinks and lunch. Nat was one of the secretaries at Prince Edward School. Later we all met up at Meikles Hotel before it was time to go back to Gwelo.

On the way we had a puncture and had no tools. Fortunately help arrived in the form a kind soul who stopped and fortunately had with him a full set of tools. We made it back by 2330hrs.

Monday 18 June

At 0800hrs we drew weapons and supplies for practical field craft exercises to take place at Kutanga, a military training area towards Que Que several miles from Gwelo.

We passed a sign saying "Unauthorized Entry Prohibited"

to arrive at a small camp in the middle of the area with brick buildings, toilets and electricity. We ate our lunch off plates on tables with table-cloths. The place was run by the Air Force and these boys really knew what was going on comfort-wise.

We settled in, and then, in the afternoon, we did exercises tearing around the bush doing section battle drills, using live rounds for the first time. The enemy needless to say was imaginary, their "position" being pointed out by the directing staff as "that clump of bushes" or "that small kopje". It required a great deal of imagination to carry out the various procedures.

In the evening we had a session on night sentry duty, with some of us being the sentries and the rest trying to get as close to them as possible without being heard or seen.

The rest of the night was spent having a long informal chat with Lieutenant McDermott and Colour Wales about the course and what was meant by leadership over a few beers. It became a little clearer where they were coming from. Although we, who were essentially civilian in our outlook, didn't necessarily agree with them, by the end we had more of an idea of what they wanted out of us. Basically, we had to be more like them.

We hit the sack at about midnight.

Tuesday 19 June

The morning saw us up early and off to the bombing area to witness a Hunter strike. The sheer speed of the strike was the thing that surprised us. One only heard the noise of the jet engines a second before the plane was over and past – it would be a terrifying experience for anyone on the receiving end.

Shortly Provosts came through sending down frantan, a euphemism for napalm, but with the same devastating effect. Then we were off to the training area to fire rifle grenades. The grenade was fixed over the muzzle of the FN and a gas cartridge placed in the breach. Colour Wales showed us how to hold the FN with the finger just grazing the trigger on firing, as the very severe kick produced by the gas cartridge could easily break one's finger.

We took turns to aim our grenades at an old car wreck about 100m away. None of us hit it, although most of us came very close, some of us nursing sore or sprained digits. Colour Wales fired the last grenade and scored an impressive bulls-eye. We all howled in derision at his luck but we could see that he was quite pleased with himself.

We moved on to experience crack and thump. We moved in sections along a narrow gulley while the directing staff fired on us, just over our heads or slightly to the left or right. We were to listen for the crack as the round went past us close by and then the thump, which was the sound of the round being fired. This phenomenon was caused by the fact that at 2800 feet per second, the round was travelling faster than the speed of sound.

We spent the rest of the day carrying out a "Drake Shoot". This was a technique for killing, immobilizing or flushing out the enemy in a suspected ambush position or temporary defensive position in thick cover or having just opened fire from thick cover. The idea was to fire at the base of likely cover. One also had to bear in mind that since most of the Shona or Ndebele people were right-handed because of their culture, for instance they would eat their food using the right hand only, concealed terrs would likely be on the right side of large objects such as trees. Dummies or cardboard cutouts were placed in wooded areas, to all intents and purposes out of sight, and we were required to fire to see if we could hit them. After several hours of this we were able to achieve a reasonable amount of success every time.

We returned home to a rugby practice and the news that the Wing Sergeant Major had been on the war-path and that both the Junior Course and the Senior Course had received shine parades for alleged irregularities at musters. In short we had escaped by not being there. God, did it ever end?

Wednesday 20 June

The morning was spent at lectures in Taungup. We covered the principles of defence and the roles of the section and platoon in defence and defence routine. In the afternoon we had an extensive session using a cloth model covering all we had done in the morning before being shown the film "A Day in the Line".

The basic principles of defence were that ground of tactical importance had to be denied to the enemy, defence locations had to be sited in depth and organized for all-round defence (the example of the defence of Singapore was cited here). They had to be mutually supporting and concealed. Counter-attack plans had to be made, communications had to be good and administration had to be carefully planned.

We were told that a platoon, in classical warfare, rarely occupied a defensive position on its own and that therefore the Platoon Commander would site his platoon to conform to the company plan. Orders from his Company Commander would therefore include tasks, arcs of fire and platoon boundaries. Commanders at all levels were to think "two down" when siting a defence position, so Platoon Commanders would site each weapon slit for the whole platoon, starting with the machine guns, then the section posts and finally platoon HQ.

The platoon tasks would then be carried out. These included posting sentries and organizing patrols in and out, with passwords being issued for returning patrols, digging, wiring, mining and setting trip flares.

A properly-organized defence routine had to be in place. This included such things as storage of equipment, dress, cleanliness of the position, cleaning weapons, personal hygiene, the siting and maintenance of latrines, the length of watches and feeding. All this information was given to us in the minutest detail, and it was very easy to spend a day on just the very basics of defence.

The evening was spent studying for the progress test to be held next day, while 130 were happily drinking in the pub. I was last into bed, mostly because I had got the hell in at about 2100hrs and ducked off for a couple of ales with 130 in the mess.

Thursday 21 June

On the shortest day of the year, a fact pointed out to us by Digby Neuhoff, we kicked off the day with a lecture from CSM Hartman on the roles and organization of the SAS.

The SAS, the Special Air Service, is a regular army covert unit designed to operate well behind enemy lines for the purpose of sabotage, reconnaissance and short sharp attacks. The original SAS was established during the desert campaign during World War Two under the command of Major David Stirling.

Rhodesian volunteers formed C Squadron during Second World War. It was disbanded and then reformed in 1962, again as C Squadron. The Rhodesian unit allowed for a squadron of 188 men plus 17 officers. The current establishment, was 163 men with 17 officers.

The squadron was currently divided up into squadron HQ, with 21 men and 3 officers, A troop and B troop, each with 56 men and 5 officers, a training troop of 7 men and 2 officers and an administration troop of 23 men and 2 officers.

The high ratio of officers to men was, due to the nature of

the operations they undertook. There were in addition attachments from the Rhodesian Signals Corps, the Rhodesian Army Service Corps and other units as needed. Soldiers could only join after some military experience in other units and then only after passing a rigid selection course.

We then had another lecture, this time on the 3.5 inch rocket launcher or bazooka, followed by a practical using dummy rockets. Its weight was 15lbs with a 3.75lb rocket. It could be sighted up to 950 yards, but its effective range was 100 yards. Its back-blast area was a triangle of 30 degrees, apex at breech, 25 yards long. Its penetration was 11 inches of armour plating. We never actually fired the Bazooka. I suppose the expense did not warrant it.

We rounded off the morning with the dreaded Progress Test 4. I went to lunch feeling that I had done OK.

The afternoon was spent with a practical in the weapon training area, learning to operate the MAG on a tripod. We covered the setting up and learned all about siting the weapon, fixed lines and arcs of fire. With a tripod the weapon could be fixed to fire on a specific target and still find that target in the dark or with poor visibility due to mist or smoke.

We were able to have a relaxed evening in the mess over a few beers before an early bed.

Friday 22 June

The day started with lectures on casualty evacuation, casevac for short. In deference to the fact that we were covering classical war, we were given the laid-down procedure for this type of warfare.

Stretcher bearers were to take the casualty to the company aid post (CAP) where morphine would be administered if necessary. A battalion ambulance would then get the casualty to the regimental aid post (RAP). Walking wounded would be sent directly to the RAP. Further treatment would take place there, and each casualty would be documented on an RA Med 26 form, which was then tied to his clothing.

Next stop would be either the field dressing station (FDS) or for the more serious casualties, the advanced dressing station (ADS). After more treatment the next stage would be casualty collection post (CCP), with the field surgery team (FST) - shades of "Mash"! - before final evacuation to hospitals.

As so often was the case during this classical war phase of training, knowing the Rhodesian Army establishment, we all wondered if we had the manpower to set up such an evacuation system along anything resembling a wide front. Again we wondered if our extensive study of classical war was in fact a bit of a waste of time. I said something along these lines. Lieutenant McDermott looked slightly irritated and insisted once again that aspects of our classical war training would be useful and that we could well be fighting a limited classical war in the future. This was something that we couldn't quite agree with. I demurred no further.

After the lecture we marched down to El Alamein, the cinema room. On arrival, in front of Intake 132, Pete Neupen made a mess of the halt and careered into Rob Mutch. Colour Wales bawled us out once we were in the cinema room for this "miss-drill", especially in front of the junior squad. Strange the pride instructors took in their courses. He really was disappointed.

The film "The Journey Back" took us through the casevac procedures. We then had a short lecture on the siting and use of anti-tank weapons. This was a follow-on from our exercise on the 3.5 inch Rocket Launcher.

The most important feature of siting was to ensure that the anti-tank weapon was defiladed from enemy observers, to hide the back-blast. The muzzle flash produced was negligible, but the flash and blast from the back of the weapon was considerable.

Also weapons were to be set up for mutual support and in depth.

We were also given the characteristics of several other anti-tank weapons, including the American 75mm Recoilless Rifle, the 120mm Wombat, the Swedish 84mm Carl Gustav and the Swedish wire-controlled Bantam missile.

The afternoon was spent on first aid. The medic Corporal who gave us the lecture was hilarious. He had us in stitches, not literally of course. He showed us pressure points useful for stopping bleeding and how to bandage various wounds. He described the issued field dressings as absolutely useless for staunching blood and recommended a large supply of bandages be carried instead. He even tried to get us to practise injecting each other but, regrettably for him, there were no takers.

So ended the week, and no guard duty! Next Monday and Tuesday were to be spent at Brady Barracks in Bulawayo at the School of Military Engineering.

At about six in the evening Digby Neuhoff and I went round to Chaplin School to see Bill Baker and Selwyn Stevens. We arrived at Coghlan House just in time to join in a braaivleis being held there to say farewell to a long-standing House Matron. Digby and I both being teachers, it was great to get into an environment we were familiar with and to forget about the Army for a while.

Bill was in charge of rugby at Chaplin and explained that they were short of a referee for one of the morning games. He asked me if I would be available to help him out. Since our rugby game was in the afternoon, I was happy to oblige.

Bill was Acting Housemaster, living in the Housemaster's residence. We had a few beers there after the braai before wending our way back to School of Infantry. It had been a great evening.

Saturday 23 June

After a leisurely breakfast I went to Chaplin and refereed the Chaplin-Milton U14A game. Once again I had the feeling that this was where I belonged, most definitely not with the Rhodesian Army.

I had lunch with John Jones, my old shamwari from the late sixties when we did athletics for the University College of Rhodesia (UCR) in Salisbury. John was Housemaster of Maitland House, an all-girls establishment! Well suited to a former Rhodesian rugby centre.

Then it was back to School of Infantry for my rugby game, School of Infantry Cadets vs RLI Recruits. At this stage 50% of the recruits in the RLI were South Africans. They looked lethal in the warm up, but somehow we managed to beat them.

Afterwards we had a few drinks in our mess with these South Africans. They told us how surprised they were at the discipline in the RLI and how even the Lance Corporals were gods. Most of them had had military experience in South Africa, where they assured us things were not so rigid.

After this I went to have a café meal with Hayden Whisken from the Medical Corps, who had been on duty at the match. He was meeting his girlfriend and we all went on to the cinema afterwards.

Sunday 24 June

This turned out to be a long day. In the morning Digby Neuhoff, Pete Nupen and I went to have nine holes of golf at the Selukwe Club. We loved Selukwe and the course. We then went back to School of Infantry to play Risco Firsts.

After the rugby, Digby and I took off in my Mazda for Bulawayo to Brady Barracks. We offloaded our cases in a dingy little barrack room and then after popping into the Naafi, all ranks, Digby and I went into town. We had a mixed grill at a café opposite the cinemas in Grey Street and then hit the Russett Room at the Selborne Hotel for a few beers. A nice coal fire was burning and I was reluctant to leave. We drove back to Brady to find that the others had forgotten to leave the key to the barrack room at the guard room as agreed and had pushed off into town! It was now 2130hrs, so we went to visit my friends the Stirlings. Digby had reservations as it was so late, but we were well received and given a beer each by an understanding Patrick Stirling.

Back to Brady, but there was still no sign of the rest of the course. It was 2330hrs, so off we went to Bulawayo again driving around looking for their cars. No luck, so it was back again to Brady. It was now 0030hrs and still no key!

Once again we headed for town, found the Lobels bakery and bought doughnuts before proceeding back to Brady. It was now 0130hrs. At this stage we met George Cornelius from our intake, now with Engineers. He let us into his barrack room, loaned us a couple of blankets and we slept on spare beds, seriously disenchanted with the rest of our course.

Monday 25 June

We were up at 0600hrs and across to our barrack room to harangue the rest of the course. It turned out that they had got home at 0200hrs. We breakfasted off tin plates – shades of Llewellin – and then took off to a lecture room to begin a very concentrated but very thorough two-day course.

Our first lecture was on the organization of the Corps of Engineers. Engineers consisted of two squadrons with a Regular Lieutenant Colonel, as Director of Engineers, in overall charge, a regular Major as OC and a Captain as Adjutant/2IC of each squadron, No. 1 Squadron based in Bulawayo and No. 2 Squadron in Salisbury.

In Bulawayo the squadron consisted of headquarters, the SME, a regular field troop, a national service field troop and an active TF field troop. In Salisbury the squadron was made up of headquarters, a regular field troop and an active TF field troop.

No. 3 Squadron, to consist of one regular field troop, was in the process of being formed. The field troops were engaged in constructing base camps, sundry new works and mine lifting, principally in the Centenary area.

We moved quickly on to the laying of wire obstacles in a

classical war situation. It was explained to us that there were natural obstacles such as rivers, very thick bush and swamps, artificial obstacles such as wire, dragons' teeth, tetrahedrons, minefields and demolished bridges and combinations of both.

Obstacles could be essentially classified as tactical and non-tactical. Tactical obstacles included anti-tank, anti-vehicle or anti-personnel. Non-tactical obstacles were used in the protection of installations, crowd control and road blocks.

We were lectured in how to put up various types of wire obstacles, in the main using Dannert wire, used during the First World War. Dannert wire was barbed wire that came in what appeared to be a coil but opened out like a concertina of circular pieces wired together.

We then had a practical session and with the successive use of spun yarn to mark the obstacle, cattle wire and metal pickets to set up the frame, wire loops to hold the Dannert wire and the Dannert wire itself, we spent two hours setting up catwire types one, two and three and a triple concertina fence. This took us through to lunch.

In the afternoon we laid a double apron fence with pickets, loops and rolls of barbed wire. The last part of the afternoon was spent on field defences, concentrating on the construction of trenches with an emphasis on revetment (methods of preventing trench walls from collapsing), the provision of overhead cover and protection with the use of wire, pickets, hessian binding, corrugated iron and soil.

Also covered was the layout of two-man, four-man and MAG trenches. This would come in handy during our defence exercise the following week.

After lectures we went to town as a course, with Colour Wales in the lead. A very pleasant evening was had by all and we were able to see Colour Wales in a different light – almost human in fact.

We first hit La Boheme (it had changed its name from The Stork Club) where we took in the "Sunset Strip" and consumed eight rounds of beers before 8 pm. We then split up and Digby and I had a mixed grill at the same place as Sunday night and then watched a movie called "The African Elephant", during which I fell asleep! Then it was off to the barracks and, amazingly, it was open. The key holder had arrived back.

Tuesday 26 June

We were up at 0700hrs, most of us nursing monumental hangovers. In my case it seemed to be aided and abetted by food poisoning; I had been sick all night.

The first of the morning's lectures was on explosive digging; how to loosen the earth using high explosives. Soil for a three foot by six foot trench could be loosened with 3 three-inch diameter holes dug to the depth required with post diggers, filled with 6 oz of plastic HE with detonators and Cordtex fuse at the bottom of each hole with mud filling up the rest of the hole.

Cordtex fuse detonated at a speed of 800 to 900 metres a second.

We then moved onto anti-tank/anti-vehicle mine warfare and the different types of minefield. Defensive (300 yards wide), barrier (600 yards wide), nuisance and even phony minefields were covered. Defensive and barrier minefields could only be authorized by Brigade Commanders, and nuisance minefields could only be laid with Army HQ permission.

We went over siting of minefields and minefield patterns consisting of clusters, rows and strips and laying drills with digging parties, carrying parties and laying parties. All minefields had to be signposted with red or white triangles and red or white writing.

The laying of mines that were not signposted was, we were told, strictly against the Geneva Convention; a fact that did not seem to trouble the terrs, who were placing them at random on dirt roads all over the place.

The last lecture was on anti-personnel mines. All types were discussed, with particular reference to those used by the communist forces during the Vietnam War. Our anti-personnel mines were detonated by the pressure exerted by a person's foot while walking, and even with a few ounces of HE were capable of blowing a leg off below the knee if boots were worn, and well above the knee if not. It was all very ugly stuff.

The afternoon was spent in the training area at Umzingwane, well outside Bulawayo, with practical demonstrations, each of us laying and setting off charges using HE, detonators and/or Cordtex. We had a demonstration on explosive digging and had to shovel out the dirt. This was amazingly effective and beat hands down the traditional method of loosening the soil with a pick. We were also shown the effect of an anti-personnel mine when a log with a boot on it was dropped onto one. The boot and the lower part of the log were blown to bits.

We were finished by 1700hrs and drove straight back to Gwelo for a few cokes and an early bed.

Wednesday 27 June

Today was probably the most relaxing so far. Guti was falling, so there was no musters and we only began lectures at 0845hrs. It was another cloth model on defence prior to next week's exercise. It was really a rehash of what we had already covered.

We then had a lecture on Orderly Room procedure. Basically this covered the procedure when a man was charged. He would be marched in to the orderly room by an NCO and charges would be read out by a junior officer. The soldier being charged would be required to plead guilty or not guilty to the senior officer, a Major at company level or a Lieutenant Colonel at battalion level.

A not guilty plea, which was extremely unusual, would result in dismissal or referral to higher authority, which could lead to a court martial. Punishments meted out at these proceedings were usually fines, extra duties, confinement to barracks or, for the much more serious offences such as accidental discharge, sleeping on guard or swearing at a superior rank, a spell in Detention Barracks in Bulawayo.

In the afternoon we played basketball against the African demonstration troops. At the end I wound up with a large, old and very smelly army jersey. Mine had been quietly removed by one of the opposition and I had "scored" his. These things are sent to try us.

John Richardson and I took off to town to Marche's Restaurant for anchovy toast and tea, a good old Rhodesian standby, before heading back to School of Infantry. Over the period of the course we often dropped in to Marche's, as had many servicemen from the Second World War onwards. My father and mother had visited it many times in the 1940s and the lady running it in 1973 had been there since then. Despite sanctions they always had a supply of Peck's anchovy paste and the toast was always thickly spread.

After supper a group of us went into town again, to the Midlands Hotel for a few quiet beers before bed. Technically we were still not supposed to leave School of Infantry without a pass, but from this time on our departure after hours seemed to be overlooked. The boom would be lifted at the gate with no questions asked and we would drive off into town. Occasionally the soldier on duty would "chuck us up" a salute which amused us greatly.

Thursday 28 June

I was up at 0600hrs for a shave, intending to do a bit of study before the day started, but decided on going back to bed until 0645hrs; so much for steely self-discipline.

We had decided to go to musters in webbing, since we were having our re-classification shoot with the FN, but Pete Nupen's webbing had "gunge" all over it and so as duty student I decided we would go in stable belts. Charlie Lenegan took exception and said that he was sick and tired of people wanting to change the arrangements. Of course he did have a point.

Most of us were feeling tired of the Army and a little "on edge". This always seemed to happen after we had temporarily relaxed away from what seemed at times to be the "bullshit" of day to day life at School of Infantry – daily musters, inspections and constant "revs".

We got by musters unscathed and drew weapons for the re-classification shoot. We had done so badly in the first one several weeks ago. This time I hoped to qualify as a marksman, despite being the duty student and having to run the whole thing. More and more responsibility was being put on the duty student as the course progressed.

The Rhodesian Army classification shoot was very thorough. The procedure was as follows.

First we zeroed the rifles at 100 yards. This involved firing rounds at a target and being told how far off the mark we were.

We would adjust the sights and fire again until we felt that the rifle was firing true. Then the classification shoot proper began.

We first fired at 100 yards. We fired 8 rounds standing with four exposures of a single target, two rounds at each exposure. Each exposure consisted of the target being raised from the butts, held for one second and then being lowered. This process was referred to as snap-shooting. We then had to fire from the sitting position with one exposure of each of three different targets randomly positioned in the butts, again two rounds with each exposure with the same timings.

We then moved out to 200 yards. We did snap-shooting from the prone position, two exposures with two rounds at each exposure, the same from the kneeling position and then from the sitting position put four rounds at a time into two separate targets with one exposure for each target.

We then moved out to 300 yards to fire from the prone position, first six rounds deliberate with no time limit into one target and then snap-shooting three rounds into each of three different targets with one exposure each.

We then proceeded to the run-down. In this we started from 200 yards. We ran to the 175-yard mark and fired four rounds into a fixed target from the kneeling position, to 150 yards to repeat the procedure, to 125 yards to do the same again and on to 100 yards to fire four rounds from the standing position. We then put a new magazine on the rifle, ran to 75 yards, fired four rounds from the standing position and moved to 50 yards to put a further six rounds into the target.

The classification was terminated with a full magazine being discharged at ten falling plates at 200 yards, any choice of firing position being allowed.

At the end we had all qualified as marksmen.

In the afternoon we had a lecture on the withdrawal from a defensive position and a chance to put a little bit of the knowledge gleaned from our sojourn at The School of Military Engineering using HE and detonators to blow holes in drums and fell small trees.

A very "military" day was of course spoilt by the fact that we had to spend a fair part of the evening cleaning not only our barrack room but our lecture room, Taungup, for the Friday inspection. The latter had not been swept for a while and since there was no light we had to do it by candle light. We hoped we had got it clean enough, as our weekend pass would depend on it.

Friday 29 June

Six things could have kept me from getting a pass this weekend. A bad musters in the morning, but we were almost up to scratch. A bad barrack room inspection, but we passed this easily. A dirty lecture room, but it seemed in good order. Weak results in Progress Test 4, but most of us passed. Rugby, yes there was a game on Saturday and I had to play. Guard duty, yes some of us were on it!

I had begun to seriously believe that it was impossible to

win in this place. Well, we thought, maybe a pass might eventuate over Rhodes and Founders after our defence exercise at the end of next week. We were all dreading this, as from all accounts hard manual labour and sleep deprivation were the order of the day.

Colour Wales was a little irritated with us, as we were reprimanded by other instructors on two occasions in his presence. Once at musters our hair was long enough to trip over, and once when marching in a squad, RSM Collyer found us sloppy. As duty student I copped an extra "rev" from our instructor.

"Sanderson, you have failed comprehensively to keep a grip of the squad!" he bellowed.

Most of the morning was spent in Ashanti with Lieutenant McDermott, using a cloth model to work painstakingly through a revision of the withdrawal in preparation for our defence exercise.

The rest of the morning and afternoon was spent on a practical tutorial on defence in the bush surrounding the School of Infantry. Most of the time we spent on siting the defence position, taking turns and doing it again and again in different areas, but we also covered defence routine, patrols and the withdrawal. This was known as a TEWT (tactical exercise without troops). It was a massive exercise lasting six hours.

As duty student, I had had to organize a haversack lunch from the kitchen for each member of the group and our instructor and course officer. I also had the presence of mind to organize a crate of cold Coke to be delivered to us in the bush at 1300hrs by my batman. It was hot, so this was appreciated by all, even our instructor, who grudgingly acknowledged that I had shown a little common sense.

We returned to our barrack room to get ready for guard duty to be told that the regular cadets had broken our Battle March record by two points. Their instructor had been challenged by the fact that a national service course had set it, while the regular cadets had been trying for some time before we had got there and he had vowed to keep them at it until they broke it. His determination paid off. At least we had held it for three weeks.

The rest of the evening was spent with the tedious routine of guard duty. A lucky few non-rugby players had obtained week-end leave.

Saturday 30 June

Since Saturday 2 June, at the end of the first week of second phase, Saturday mornings had been designated as "at the course officer's disposal". This meant that he could make us train, but so far, this had not happened and we had always had at least a morning pass to Gwelo.

I drove into Gwelo at about 0900hrs, had a haircut and then went to buy a few things. As I was coming out of a shop, I bumped into a former pupil of mine, Keith Spence, whom I had taught at Prince Edward the previous year. We went over to

Marche's Café and had some tea and toast and chatted. It turned out that he was on a PTC (Pilot Training Course) at Thornhill and was doing very well, especially on the academic side.

In the afternoon I played for School of Infantry Second XV against Gwelo Sports Club at School of Infantry. We won 26-6, although I didn't play very well.

After the game both teams had a few drinks in the national service mess and we got to know a few more of the blokes in Intake 132. Pete Arnold and Mike Lambiris I knew from Prince Edward. They had left in 1968, the year before I started teaching there, but I had met them many a time in the Prince Edward pub when they had returned to visit their former English teacher Mike Clarke. After his training at Gwelo Mike Lambiris joined me at my unit.

Sunday 1 July

Today was a very quiet one, spent catching up on notes from SME and studying for exams on tactics, weapon training, field craft, voice procedure and map reading which were due to be written in eight days' time. We also got our kit ready for the looming defence exercise. As well as the required personal equipment, I had decided to put a few tins of bully beef as extra rations in my pack. Strictly this was an illegal move.

John Richardson and I spent the evening slowly and sedately drinking a few beers at the Cecil Hotel in a quiet bar with a coal fire, very pleasant. Unfortunately, a week with some hardship lay ahead.

Monday 2 July

The morning was spent loading all the equipment needed for the defence exercise. The list was endless. We loaded items such as sand bags, picks, shovels, Dannert wire, landmines (in reality cylinders of concrete), flares, blank ammunition, sheets of corrugated iron, pickets and hessian binding.

We were to join up with the regular cadets on the exercise, named, appropriately as it turned out, "True Grit". The regulars were already out in the exercise area siting the defensive position.

We left Gwelo at about 1400hrs and arrived at the exercise area near Selukwe at about 1515hrs. We debussed about two miles from our defensive position and were given our initial appointments, to last until next day.

I was to be a "Rifleman". We were given orders by a regular cadet, playing the part of "Platoon Commander". He did quite a good job following the laid-down procedure. After the basic ground, situation and mission, he moved onto execution and covered times by which positions had to be ready (by sunset on Tuesday), type and number of trenches to be dug, concealment and protection, sentries and alarm schemes (usually initiating fire).

As usual, the directing staff, Lieutenant McDermott, Colour Wales and others, watched the orders and took notes. We were to be No 1 Platoon together with the regular cadets. The rest of the company was imaginary.

We then walked all the way in, carrying as much equipment as we could, with the "Platoon Commander" leading. It was possible to have got there by RL, as the RL drove right up to our defensive position to offload all the equipment we had not been able to carry, but the DS wanted authenticity – we were told that in the First World War all equipment was carried into the trenches.

We started digging at 1700hrs. I had to dig a two man trench with Paul Hopcroft, a regular cadet who I had been paired up with. This was hard work.

A two-man trench was supposed to be in two parts, each six feet by two feet in area, joining each other at 135 degrees. The depth was to be at least five feet with further height protection provided by parapets made from the excavated dirt rising above the lip of the trench. Between the lip of the trench and the parapet there had to be a berm, a flat area 12 inches wide. In addition one of the six by two feet areas had to have OHP (overhead protection) using wooden beams and corrugated iron, as a sleeping bay.

It was pitch black, only starlight to see by, and at one stage a dark figure loomed up from the direction of the trench nearby, which was being dug by Beefy Barlow. We had visited each other a couple of times during the night to see how the other was progressing.

"Hello Beefy", I said, "How are you going?"

"Actually this isn't Beefy. This is your friendly Captain speaking," said a disembodied voice.

It turned out that it was Captain Fawcett playing the part of "Company Commander" as well as DS for the duration of the exercise. He was inspecting the work so far. We were told we would dig until well after midnight. During the course of the evening all the two of us had to eat or drink was a shared tin of bully beef and water from our water bottles.

Tuesday 3 July

We were awake at 0430hrs, having been made to dig until 0200hrs. We walked about half a mile to the rear to the feeding point and were given a haversack lunch consisting of two bits of bread and an orange each to last us the whole day. I thanked my lucky stars that I had brought extra food. We began digging again as soon as we got back. Surprisingly I had not developed any blisters as yet.

At 0630hrs Paul Hopcroft and I were told that our trench had been badly sited and that we had to move to higher ground about 40 yards away on a small granite kopje. We were told that we would have to build a sanga, as it was too rocky to dig a trench. We felt more than a little irritated as we had almost completed our digging, but we had by now learnt to obey and shrug our shoulders in resignation.

Sangas were supposed to be constructed out of sand bags on ground that was virtually all rock to a height of about six feet with the same dimensions and configuration as a trench with the OHP on top of the sand bags. We had had no instruction as to how to do this, but started filling the sand bags and placing them in what we thought were the correct positions. After three hours we felt that we were making good progress; certainly the sanga was taking shape a lot more quickly than our trench had.

At 1000hrs we had appointment changes. I was made a "Corporal" in charge of a trench and had to move to another sanga which was not nearly as advanced as my old one. This time I was with John Vos, another regular Cadet, and yet again set to work. At about 1200hrs our work was interrupted and we were told to move forward from our defensive position to lay land mines (the concrete slabs) for a couple of hours. You haven't lived until you have spent two hours burying cement blocks in hard ground!

Then it was back to the sanga, which we completed to the grudging approval of Captain Fawcett by about 1800hrs. We then attended orders given by the new "Platoon Commander", another regular cadet, no doubt passing on information that had been given to him by Captain Fawcett. The orders took the usual format but in addition, this time, he covered arcs of fire, times of stand to, section boundaries and patrol timings and composition.

That night's recce patrol was then detailed off for further

orders. I wasn't included, but word was sent by messenger from trench to trench to give patrol timings, that is to say when they would be leaving, the passwords for the returning patrol and route out and in. The time of their return was obviously flexible.

We were told to expect an initial attack sometime that night. The part of the "enemy" would be played by DS and African demonstration troops.

Having had two hours' sleep since Monday morning John and I were feeling pretty "bushed" and the prospect of being on watch and watch, one on guard while the other slept, did not appeal, but it had to be done. Also, the fact that both of us would have to be awake for each simulated attack did not make things better. The only consolation was that any sleep we managed to snatch would be deep.

Wednesday 4 July

During the night, to our great surprise, we got a reasonable amount of sleep. Maybe the directing staff were having a bit of a party. In any event, apart from the patrol coming back, a few jitter patrols in the form of shadowy figures coming close to our trenches and then melting away as we opened fire and a couple of bombardments (thunder-flashes let off near our trenches) nothing much happened. The "enemy" had arrived.

We were up at 0500hrs and off to the feeding point to collect another haversack lunch, exactly the same as the one we had got the previous day. We then lay in our trenches until about 1000hrs, when appointments were changed again.

Once again I was made a "Rifleman" and plonked in a new trench in the right forward part of our defensive sector. This time only a little bit of work had to be done on the position. Once again I had been paired with a regular Cadet, Tony Hurlbatt. He had spent one year at the Teachers' College in Bulawayo before coming to School of Infantry.

The thing about defence was that once positions were set up, boredom set in. There was time to talk about the training and the relative merits of teaching and soldiering.

The regular cadets had a course lasting just over a year whereas we national servicemen crammed all our training into 19 weeks. I joked that we only needed 19 weeks because we were more intelligent, but in reality their course was much more thorough and detailed.

Part of the discussion was about the appointments for the next day. Neither of us fancied the idea of being made "Platoon Commander" and having to deal with the withdrawal. This would mean having to recce the withdrawal route, giving extensive orders, successfully leading the platoon out of the position in the pitch dark to awaiting vehicles to take us away and siting a new defensive position.

During the afternoon we were once again detailed off to lay landmines for an hour or so. So far there had been no visitations from DS to the minefield and one of the regular cadets, an American, decided to lie down, take his shirt off and sunbathe for a few minutes. Unfortunately, as often happens, a member of the directing staff came out of the bush and caught him in the act. There was a fair amount of gnashing of teeth and tearing of hair, with unspecified retribution promised before the DS went on his way. At 1600hrs some of us were detailed off to form a fighting patrol to move out about an hour after last light. Once again I wasn't included but this time, as well as the usual patrol information, the messenger told us that the regular cadet who had been sunbathing would be doing the patrol without a shirt with only his webbing to keep him warm. We collectively winced. On all our night exercises we had seriously felt the cold wearing a vest, shirt, jersey and combat jacket, especially when lying still.

The night was in sharp contrast to the previous one, I only managed to snatch an hour's sleep in total. Our patrol went out. Routes out and in were just past our trench, and then the fun started.

There were constant jitter patrols for a few hours then, after the patrol returned, a loudspeaker system, which seemed to operate at about a million decibels, started to blare forth enemy propaganda.

Statements along the lines of "Give up and you will be treated well" abounded, followed by threats of what would happen to us if we did not give up. Some statements claimed that Captain Fawcett had been captured and he was tortured all night with commentary, given in explicit detail, on what was being done to him. His screams, or those of a stand-in, carried on for several hours.

Sandwiched in between broadcasts we had an infiltration patrol, that is to say an "enemy" patrol pretending to be one of ours. Unfortunately for them it chose our trench to pass by and, since we had already seen our patrol in, we were able to open up on them straightaway with the nearby trenches joining in. This was at least one good mark for the cadets.

Thursday 5 July

Once again there was the 0430hrs trip to the feeding point to get rations and then back to the bloody trenches to sit, filthy dirty, cold, generally bored and fed up. The exercise was obviously designed to simulate as far as possible life in a defensive position and seemed to be succeeding in this. The food, in particular, was inadequate and always cold and we had finished my last tin of corned beef during the night.

At about 0800hrs mail was brought to the trenches, which cheered us up enormously. I spent a few minutes reading letters from friends Bill Cock and Cynthia Edwards.

At 1000hrs I was able to heave a sigh of relief as, when the new appointments were handed out, I had been made a "Section Commander". All I had to do was concentrate on alarm systems, arcs of fire and making sure that everyone kept in their trenches.

Trench latrines had been dug behind the trenches, but we were only supposed to use them at night to avoid being "fired on" while in the open. This was one occasion when I turned a blind eye to regulations, left the trench and visited the trench latrine as needed during the day after a quick check to see if the DS were anywhere near. So did others. There were limits, I felt, to this playing soldiers business.

If caught, I had resolved to say that I had used the crawl trenches that technically were supposed to have been dug between positions for communication. This probably would have got me into trouble for being a "smart arse", but I was beyond caring. Luckily for me I was not spotted.

Keith Lindsay was appointed "Platoon Commander" and at 1415hrs was taken off for a briefing at D Company Command Post and a recce of the withdrawal route. He returned at about 1600hrs and gave orders to an orders group, consisting of the "Platoon 2I/C" and the "Section Commanders", in his trench. I suppose we must have pretended to use the non-existent crawl trenches to get there.

I thought he did quite well but, as was now expected, he copped a "rev" from our course officer nevertheless for lack of clarity and leaving things out. We then went back to relay the orders to our sections. The withdrawal was due to start about an hour after the return of the night patrol.

We waited in our trenches, wide awake, coping with all the

jitter patrols and loudspeaker propaganda until the return of the patrol, then began the withdrawal at 2400hrs. It went much as we had feared it would. Keith had been taken over the withdrawal route in broad daylight and it was complicated, with similar boulders and masasa trees at every turn. In the darkness it was almost impossible to retrace, and we became hopelessly lost. I was convinced that none of us would have done any better than Keith, but this fact did not stop Captain Fawcett, who was following Keith closely, becoming apoplectic. Apparently he had not been "captured".

I was just behind leading number one section and watched the whole performance. He screamed and ranted at Keith for about five minutes, questioning everything from his ability to his ancestry before angrily showing him the way. I felt that the whole thing was ridiculously overdone and achieved nothing other than to completely demoralize those who witnessed it. It did not make us better soldiers.

To this day, I cannot see the logic in the severity of the criticism directed at Keith. Certainly any shreds of enthusiasm that Keith might have had for the Army dissipated that night. I wasn't too wild about it either at that moment. Many of us could have failed this particular task and in my opinion a short sharp admonishment would have sufficed.

Friday 6 July

We found our way to the transport at about 0200hrs and were carted, freezing on the back of our RL, 10 miles back along the road to be ordered to dig in again. Captain Fawcett took over the siting of the new trenches. Orders were to reach 4 foot 6 inches by first light. We were all very tired by now and most of us had only made about two feet in the rocky ground as it became light.

Captain Fawcett had been hinting as we worked that we would keep digging until lunchtime if we did not reach the required depth, but at 0630hrs he called the exercise off with the words "It's over gentlemen". What a relief those words brought.

We proceeded to fill in the recently-dug trenches, then it was back to the original defence position feeding point to receive a terrific mixed grill, hot and wholesome. We then cleared our defensive position of "mines" and wire, emptied sand bags and filled in trenches. We arrived back at the School of Infantry in time to hand in equipment and grab a quick shower and lunch.

After lunch we, along with the regular cadets, had an introductory lecture from a Captain Clewer on COIN (Counter Insurgency) with an accompanying Sitrep (Situation Report) on the current state of the war. We were dog-tired and had to fight hard to stay awake. The Sitrep seemed to indicate that in the Hurricane area (the north eastern part of Rhodesia) we had had a few successes, with some kills, although landmines had destroyed several army and civilian vehicles, which resulted in five people being killed with quite a few more injured.

We finished the day with a pay parade and changed into civvies to go on leave for the Rhodes and Founders weekend. Digby Neuhoff, myself and John Richardson took turns to drive to Salisbury. I fell exhausted into bed at Eddie and Rena Mooney's house at about 2100hrs.

During my time at Gwelo a host of people offered me a place to stay while on leave. I was very grateful for this.

Saturday 7 July

The Rhodes and Founders weekend, from Saturday to Tuesday inclusive, was, for me, going to be spent seeing friends and studying for the three massive exams to be written on the Wednesday straight after the holiday. These were a written tactics exam, a practical weapon training and field-craft exam and a voice procedure and map reading exam.

I spent Saturday morning in Salisbury doing some shopping. In town I bumped into several people I knew, Iain Bowen, Laurie Rickards (School of Infantry), and Manley Palmer. I had not seen Iain since 1969, when I met him along with Mick Graham when they were stationed with the SAS in a camp near Mana Pools. They had taken me for a ride in a Land Rover, ostensibly on patrol but in reality for a bit of game spotting. I remember at one stage being in the middle of a herd of wildebeest on the stampede. Manley Palmer had just left Prince Edward with his RCE Upper Level and was an apprentice electrician.

I spent the whole of the afternoon doing a bit of study before a great Chinese meal at the Golden Dragon with Ed and Rena in the evening.

Sunday 8 July

The morning and early afternoon were spent on a long walk down the upper Mazoe valley and back. No water in the upper reaches, as far as I walked, compared with the previous summer when there had been a substantial flowing stream after the very late rains. It was great to be walking in the Rhodesian bush without having to carry a nine pound FN and webbing.

The evening was spent visiting Leigh and Elizabeth Lautenbag together with their children Wayne and Leanne. It was a tremendous evening with great food and excellent company. It turned out that they were friends with Major Mike Shute, 2 IC School of Infantry.

Monday 9 July

The morning was spent studying. I then went for lunch with

Mike and Ann Clarke. Mike was Head of English at Prince Edward and we had been on a few fishing trips to Kariba over the years. He was a member of a syndicate of three people owning a sixteen foot ski-boat called appropriately *Cindykate* and lovingly maintained by Graham Longhurst a member of the syndicate. It was great fun remembering funny stories of trips to Charara and the Sanyati Gorge and getting an update on Prince Edward School.

The evening was spent with Keith Corbett, my former boss in the Mathematics Department at Prince Edward School, and his family. In the course of the evening, I learnt, for the first time, that he had been wounded in the shoulder during the Second World War in the Italian campaign. Keith was an amazing man and one of the best Mathematicians I have known. He was a graduate from Cambridge, I suspect a wrangler, and had taught at Prince Edward since 1954.

Tuesday 10 July

The whole morning was spent studying. It seemed a shame that a perfectly good holiday morning should be ruined by work. I visited my parents and had a quick run with the dog in the afternoon before dropping in to see the sisters at the Prince Edward School hospital. A new boy, William Light, was in hospital with the flu. I knew his father and mother, Buddy and Joan, very well, having stayed with the Lights on their farm near Mt Darwin a few days before starting National Service.

I picked up Digby Neuhoff for the trip back to Gwelo. John was making his own way back. We decided by way of a change to go back via Umvuma instead of taking the Bulawayo road. Not being in a frantic hurry to get back to the School of Infantry, we dropped in at the Enkeldoorn Hotel for a drink.

We were served in the bar by Henry Cook, who had run the place for some years. Memories surfaced of the incredible hospitality that he had given me and five others in 1967, as members of a group of students from the University College of Rhodesia who were pushing a wheelbarrow full of manure from Enkeldoorn to Salisbury as a rag stunt to raise money for charity. We had gone up on a Friday evening and he had put all of us up gratis in his hotel and had started us off with his shotgun early on Saturday morning with a selection of Afrikaans Enkeldoorn residents looking on incredulously with comments such as "Wat maak hulle?" ("What are they doing?") and "Is hulle mal of iets?" ("Are they mad or something?") delivered with a sense of bewilderment. We had played Bok-Bok with the particularly hefty local farmers in the bar the previous night with the aid of a few drinks, and I remember that we were feeling fairly shattered.

His hospitality had not abated. As soon as he heard that we were in the Army he gave us our first drink free. Another customer offered us another drink and then another. When it came to our turn they refused absolutely point blank to accept a drink from us. We finally got back to Gwelo, after a bit of carburettor trouble, at close to 0100hrs on Wednesday.

Wednesday 11 July 1973.

We got through musters without any drama and moved onto Taungup for our exams. The tactics exam was more difficult than I had expected, but the weapon training and field-craft exams were reasonable.

We went into lunch, where we met the senior intake, Intake 130, who had been given their appointments. There was a mixed atmosphere of elation and disappointment amongst them, depending on the rank they had been given. They had done very well, with seven of them being commissioned.

After offering congratulations or commiserations, we moved off to write the voice procedure and map reading exam, which also turned out to be relatively easy, winding up at 1600hrs. We went in early to the mess to have a few drinks with 130. Rob Mutch drew attention to the fact that once 130 had left on Saturday, we would be the senior intake. It was interesting to reflect that this had happened very quickly. We noted that the next day, as we were entering the third phase of our training and COIN, it would be exactly three months since we had entered the Army. We wondered if we would get special treatment as a result of our new status.

After supper I went to visit Bill Baker for a couple of drinks before going out to Gwelo Sports Club with Selwyn Stevens, as he was a member, for a few more. This was all still technically breaking bounds.

I met up with Vance Carlisle, brother of Alistair Carlisle, whom I knew. Both were Prince Edward old boys, before my time at the school. We discussed many of the teachers who had taught him and who were still there.

In particular we talked about Rex McCulloch. Vance obviously thought the world of him. Rex was an amazing character, possibly the most charismatic person I have known, and a brilliant Geography teacher and schoolmaster. His physical appearance was itself almost intimidating. He was a big man with bushy black kinesthetic eyebrows. He had a devastating sense of humour and could tell the funniest stories, always with an absolutely straight face, while everyone around him was doubling up with laughter. When he did find something totally hilarious the most I saw him muster up, by way of appreciation, was a sort of gapped-tooth grimace. He was a strong disciplinarian but, he was also one of the kindest and generous men I ever met.

Thursday 12 July 1973.

It had been unwise to have a late night as we were up at 0600hrs for a three-mile road run. After the dreaded musters (not so dreaded as it was taken by Colour Wales since Sergeant Major

Hallamore was away), we moved onto Taungup for lectures from an Inspector from the BSAP. Policing had an important role in counter insurgency throughout the war, particularly in the urban areas.

The first lecture was on the organisation and role of the British South Africa Police (BSAP). The BSAP at that time consisted almost entirely of regulars with the civilian elements of PATU (Police Anti-Terrorist Unit) who were mostly rural and the Special Constabulary, a mostly urban neighbourhood watch organization. Just recently, a decision had been made to take national servicemen into the BSAP, as was happening with the RLI, because of a lack of regular volunteers.

We were given a fascinating and humorous first-hand account of the day-to-day life of a policeman and a personal step-by-step account of the career of our lecturer, from his days training at Depot to his experiences in Salisbury and posting as member in charge of a rural police station.

He was a little disparaging about the lack of border security information being passed on to the police via Internal Affairs. This was an attitude prevailing amongst most of the Rhodesian Security Force personnel and a great deal of the blame for the initial undetected incursions by terrorists in the north-east was laid on Internal Affairs. Having spent a short amount of time in Internal Affairs, I could to a certain extent see his point but was always convinced that the BSAP were far more to blame for this lack of intelligence.

I can remember a conversation in the Jam Jar, the BSAP pub in Kariba, when I was in Internal Affairs in early 1973. The member in charge, Ian Taylor, asked me about intelligence gathering with regard to terrorist incursions in the Omai Tribal Trust Lands. I replied that as far as I knew there were no incursions but that I was relying on interpreters to question chiefs and elders about this and that the District Officer, who was fluent in Shona, Theo Kaschula, had been seconded to the military for several months. Unfortunately this answer was not received with much enthusiasm by anyone. I remember Rick Powell, who was a cashier at the Standard Bank in Kariba, being particularly scathing about Internal Affairs not doing their job properly and, by association, both me and our District Commissioner, Don Aylward. Their definition of what my job should be differed considerably from what I thought it to be.

At that time Internal Affairs had as their number one priority the development and well-being of the Africans in the TTLs (Tribal Trust Lands). We were not as yet a paramilitary organization. As an Internal Affairs Cadet I had gone on un-armed fortnightly trips, with African messengers as interpreters, to the four areas in the Omai Tribal Trust Lands. These were Nebiri, Mola, Sampakaruma and Negande. We would meet the Chiefs and elders and ask them questions on such things as their crop situations, land development and civil disputes and try to provide solutions. We would also, at length, question them about any strangers in the area and any suspicious or unusual happenings.

During my time in the Omai TTLs there was nothing to report and in fact, as it turned out, there was no terrorist activity, but I wonder if we would have heard much if there had in fact been terrorists in the area. The four Chiefs were paid $150 a month by the government, delivered by me in cash. Most people knew this and consequently one of the terrorist tactics was to discredit the Chiefs as Government stooges. Quite a bit of information would have been withheld from the Chiefs and the Chiefs themselves, in many cases, would have been intimidated to remain silent.

The police, on the other hand, when on patrol had as one of their priorities border control. They were supposed to establish a network of locals who could inform them of terrorist activity. Where was that intelligence in the north east?

One thing was clear. The roles of the BSAP were hugely diverse, from urban policing to border control with motorized patrols, and their numbers were being stretched doing all this. To overcome this discrepancy there was a move, especially in the rural areas, to combine certain operations with the military.

The second lecture consisted of how the police and the military would combine during cordon and search and road block operations. The implementation of these procedures turned out to be more complicated than one would at first expect and required a great deal of preparation. The lecture focused on what would happen at grass roots level, with practical lessons on how to search a suspect. We all practised on each other. It also focused on how to search a room and how to physically set up a road block. The rest of the morning was spent operating a road block in the training area, using African demonstration troops in civvies as suspects.

In the afternoon we travelled to the Police Dog Training Centre at Senka and watched demonstrations on how they were used for arrests and for tracking. It was all most interesting.

In the evening I drove over to Thornhill School to see a production of "Oliver". It was very well done, with a master playing Fagin and the part of Oliver being played by a boy called Stephen Prophit. Both were excellent.

At the interval I met up with Ron Reeves-Johnson, with whom I had taught at Gifford in 1969, and John Eadie, Headmaster of Thornhill, who had taught me Geography at Mt Pleasant in the early sixties.

Friday 13 July

We took an early breakfast and then it was onto an RL for the journey to Thornhill Air Base to be given an insight into the organisation and roles of the Rhodesian Air Force and the types of aircraft and weaponry available for operations. We were ushered into a lecture room, all very informal unlike the Army, and given a talk on the organisation of the Rhodesian Air Force and on Thornhill in particular.

In 1973 there were two main air bases in Rhodesia, one at

New Sarum in Salisbury, adjoining Salisbury Airport, and one at Thornhill in Gwelo. It was at these that all the training, ground and flight, took place, where all major maintenance was carried out and where most ordinance was stored.

There were other permanent air bases located elsewhere such as Grand Reef near Umtali. RAF New Sarum consisted of the main communications centre, Number 1 Ground Training School (GTS), Pilot Training School (PTS) and Numbers 3 (Douglas C-47s), 5 (Canberras) and 7 (Alouettes) Squadrons.

RAF Thornhill consisted of Number 2 Ground Training School, Pilot Training School and Numbers 1 (Hawker Hunters), 2 (Vampires), 4 (Trojans) and 6 (Provosts) Squadrons.

Number 1 Ground Training School (New Sarum) was for the technical training of young engineering recruits but in addition provided the infrastructure for Officers' Administration courses.

Number 2 GTS (Thornhill) was responsible mainly for initial officer training, including the Initial Training School (ITS) and the co-ordination with No 6 Squadron in relation to Basic Flying School (BFS) and the Advanced Flying School (AFS).

We were given a bewildering chain of command diagram for the organisation of Rhodesian Air Force Thornhill. To reduce it all to the basics there was first of all a Station OC with a Station Adjutant. Then there was a Flying Wing OC and Adjutant, a Technical Wing OC and Adjutant and an Administration Wing OC.

The flying wing incorporated the four squadrons, flying control, the GTS, an operations centre, a meteorology centre and the Kutanga firing range.

The technical wing was hugely complicated, incorporating motor transport, aircraft components, electrical equipment maintenance and installation, workshops, signals and radio maintenance, air photography, armament, safety equipment and ground equipment. The administration wing was responsible for pay and accounting. The organization at New Sarum was much the same.

We were then taken on a tour of the base and shown pretty much all that had been explained to us in the lecture. It was a very impressive and slickly-operated place. A statistic that stuck in our minds was that the Rhodesian Air Force could mobilise 97% of its aircraft, fixed wing or helicopters, at any time, a figure that no other Air Force in the world could match.

We went back to School of Infantry in time for lunch before afternoon lectures on GAC (Ground Air Control), basically the procedure for radio contact between aircraft and ground troops. GAC could also stand for ground–air controller.

The first stage of GAC involved the contact and homing of the aircraft to an overhead position. If, after a patrol made initial contact with terrorists, an air attack was deemed necessary, a radio message would be sent to their unit's base as part of a contact report, given in clear transmission, with a request for air support included.

Base would then be responsible for getting aircraft airborne and heading in the general direction of the patrol's location. The ground-air controller, usually the patrol leader, would then listen on channels 1, 2 or 3 depending on which brigade area 1, 2 or 3 one was operating in. The pilot would initiate radio contact and ask for a channel change if needed.

Aircraft were fitted with homing devices, and 20-second unmodulated transmissions, involving the ground-air controller continuously pressing the prestle switch, would help guide it in.

As the aircraft approached, the GAC would give the grid reference of his position and, very importantly, the bearing and distance of the terrorist position from his own. Once the aircraft was visual, instructions such as "go left" and "roll out" could be used to guide it to an overhead position.

The second stage was the indication of FLOT (forward line of own troops). This involved some sort of smoke indication using orange, red or yellow mini flares or white phosphorus grenades. The pilot would then say either "FLOT visual" or "Negative FLOT please re-mark." It was interesting to note that the Air Force used the word "please".

The third stage was the indication of the target.

This could be done by firing a flare or smoke grenade in the direction of the enemy position or using the clock ray method with the FLOT being given the 9 o'clock to the 3 o'clock position and the enemy position being 10, 11, 12, 1 or 2 o'clock.

The fourth stage was the aircraft attack.

In the event of a mistake, the aircraft coming in away from the enemy position or anything else, the GAC was to say "Stop, stop, stop" and the attack would be aborted. After each strike the GAC was to give corrections such as "add 50 yards" or "left 50 yards" for subsequent strikes. The GAC and pilot were to report on the effects of each attack.

In the evening the whole course went for more than a few drinks at the Midlands Hotel.

Saturday 14 July

We assembled for lectures feeling a little the worse for wear, conscious of the fact that we were not getting the morning off this Saturday. The lectures were on COIN Command and Control, followed by an introduction to patrols in COIN operations.

Right at the top the Government Cabinet formulated policy and the Security Co-ordinating Committee (SCC), essentially consisting of the PM, the Minister of Defence, the Chief of Staff, the heads of the Army, Air Force and Police with sundry advisors, processed it. To assist them at a more local level with Internal Security Operations (ISOPS), there were Provincial Civil Defence Co-ordinating Committees and District Civil Defence Committees. The former consisted of the Provincial Commissioner (PC), the Provincial OC of the BSAP, the Army

Commander, usually a Brigadier, the Air Force Commander and a permanent secretary.

The latter consisted of the District Commissioner (DC), senior Army, Air Force and BSAP officials and often CID, farmers, game rangers and the like.

COIN (Counter Insurgency) operations, military in nature and within the country, were dealt with by JOCs (Joint Operation Centres) throughout the country, consisting of Senior Army, Air Force and BSAP officers, including SB and CID representatives. By invitation DCs, LDOs (Land Development Officers), game rangers, farmers and the like could attend meetings which took place daily.

Central intelligence organisation was in the hands of Joint Planning Staff (JPS) and Operations Co-ordinating Committee (OCC), consisting of very senior security force personnel, answerable to and reporting to the SCC.

Attention had been given to psychological operations with the creation of a PSYOPS Committee answerable to the SCC.

After a tea break, Colour Wales took over from Lieutenant McDermott. This was a relatively easy task for Colour Wales as this was one area in which the procedure for COIN was very similar to that for classical war. Essentially we covered patrol formations, silent signals and patrol briefing and de-briefing.

Lectures over, Pete Addison and I made a lightning trip to Salisbury. After dropping him off at the George Hotel, I spent the afternoon watching the rugby game between UCT and Old

Boys and then arrived at Ed and Rena Mooney's place to spend the night. Once again it was great to spend an evening with old friends.

Sunday 15 July

I celebrated my 26th birthday very quietly, with a lazy morning followed by a game of golf on the police golf course in the afternoon. After a few drinks and an evening meal with Ed and Rena I made my way to pick up Pete Addison at 2000hrs at the George. After a quick drink we decided to go and see "Hitler's Last 10 Days", which was showing at the Seven Arts Theatre just across the road. This resulted in our arriving in Gwelo at 0230hrs.

Monday 16 July

The morning's lectures, given by Lieutenant McDermott, were on the ambush. Apparently, so far, the greatest number of terrorist kills had been attained through ambush and so quite a bit of time would be spent on this.

Ambushes could be laid as a result of intelligence, chance information and appreciation. The principles of ambush were good shooting, careful planning and briefing, good security, intelligent layout and siting, concealment, determination to wait and kill and a clear-cut plan. Ambushes were to be laid out in depth to cut all routes in and out.

Killer groups, in the immediate area of the ambush, consisted of two men each with stop groups to prevent escape, consisting of three men each. All groups had to enter their positions from the rear and all traces of moving in and out were to be destroyed.

The commander of the ambush would have to have a full view of the killing ground and be positioned for maximum control. Fire positions of all groups were to cover a maximum field of fire. Plans had to be made for the taking up of new positions if needed after springing the ambush.

The first part of laying an ambush was recce and planning. To do this one had to consider intelligence, clearance from appropriate authority, time available, security and the ground.

After adequate planning, highly-detailed orders had to be given to all members of the ambush party. If possible an extra briefing in the ambush area had to take place. Simulated rehearsals as to how to approach the ambush area and order of occupying killing and ambush positions group by group had to be carried out.

Before leaving for the ambush a stringent inspection of equipment had to be carried out by the commander. When springing the ambush, range had to be kept to a minimum, a contingency plan had to be in operation to allow stop groups to initiate the ambush if the terrorists did not reach the killing ground, at night illumination and fire had to be simultaneous, a cease-fire signal had to be given and MAGs had to be with killer groups.

Finally, after some time spent in the ambush positions after the ambush, a laid-down search pattern for terrorists and weapons had to be initiated. This could involve the use of trackers.

Ambushes failed because of noise, high shooting, movement at the crucial time, footprints, command badly situated and lack of all-round observation.

After a tea break the last lecture before lunch was on the details of actually giving orders. There was so much to cover, as not the least detail could be left out.

As with most orders the main headings were situation, mission, execution, administration and logistics and command and signals, but it was under the headings of execution, administration and logistics and command and signals that the real detail was contained. Without a doubt these were the most comprehensive orders that we had yet come across.

After lunch we had a lecture plus slide show on terrorist small arms weapons. We looked at the AK automatic rifle, the SKS single shot rifle, the RPD machine gun and the 7.62 Tokarev pistol. We then moved onto the 30-yard range to actually fire a few rounds from each weapon. They seemed quite effective and robust, but with shorter rounds and shorter barrels they did not have the hitting power or the accuracy of our FN and MAG.

We finished off the day with two colour films recently made in Rhodesia, "Ambush" and "Ground Air Control", which augmented what we had just learnt.

The mood in the mess was much more positive than it had been for quite a while. We all felt that at last we were being trained for something that we would actually be doing.

Tuesday 17 July

The morning was spent in the School of Infantry training area.

We first did a recce of the ambush area, with each of us having to choose our own layout in case we were chosen to be the one to give the ambush orders.

We then went back to the School of Infantry, prepared our orders and then constructed a model of the ambush area in the school sand-pit. Charlie Lenegan was chosen to give the orders.

After making some additions to the sand-pit model he gave what I thought were good orders. Inevitably, though, there was always criticism from the DS and Charlie had a few omissions volubly pointed out to him. In particular it was pointed out that he had failed to give a password and had not got us to synchronize watches.

Once again though, as we talked at lunch the mood was buoyant, and we felt that we were really learning things that were relevant.

The first hour of the afternoon was spent having an administration lecture on Q Accounting. Basically this covered how to obtain rations and equipment and how to keep a record of transactions. The lecturer was Staff Sergeant Pearce from the

Army Services Corp attached to Cadet Wing. We were given the details of how to obtain rations, clothing, weapons, ammunition and explosives and expendables at the platoon level. We were to "watch stores like a hawk!" and check them every day.

Most of the Q Accounting at company level was done by the CQMS, but it was necessary for platoon leaders to be familiar with these procedures and the requisite forms for various items. In company base they would have to deal with the CQMS. There were quite a number of these forms and we were assailed with the RA/Q/34, RA/Q/1179, RA/Q/183, RA/Q/88, Z828T, Z4, Z132T and the magic and, soon to become very familiar, RA/Q/1033.

At the end of the lecture, Staff Sergeant Pearce spilt the beans by saying that when we were in the field the 1033 would cover most contingencies. This was certainly true and most Rhodesians serving in the war used a 1033 at some time.

For the last part of the afternoon we were given a debrief on our mid-course examinations. As expected, the tactical examination results were the least impressive, but our voice procedure/map reading and weapon training/field-craft examinations results were quite good.

The highest overall mark was 79% and the lowest 55%. Lieutenant McDermott was less alarmed about the results than usual, which meant either he was secretly quite pleased or had totally given up on us.

We had a quiet evening, with a few beers and a relatively early bed.

Wednesday 18 July

We were up at 0530hrs for a road run, supposedly to be taken by Lieutenant McDermott. He didn't arrive, so we went for a short run anyway. Such was the resolution of the Rhodesian Officer Cadet! The lectures due to be taken by Lieutenant McDermott were taken by Colour Wales.

The first lecture was on the siting and maintenance of platoon bases from which patrols could be released. First the Platoon Commander, with a small section, would recce the area, either on foot or by vehicle, for a suitable base site. He would base his siting on good radio communications, all-round defence, availability of water, avoidance of populated areas (a difficult ask if operating in the tribal trust lands), hard standing, avoidance of game trails and ease of resupply.

Then he would bring his platoon in, indicate a 12 to 6 o'clock line and using this, detail positions to each section or group. A stand-to would then be ordered and 360-degree security patrol sent out.

The commander would then check and adjust positions for all groups and then make out orders while waiting for the return of the patrol. Orders would be similar to those for a classical war defensive position, but with an emphasis on self-reliance.

Most supplies and water would have to be obtained by the platoon itself as in COIN, independent operation was the norm. There would also be much more patrolling. Constant 360-

degree security patrols as well as search patrols would have to be sent out.

The next two lectures were on encounter action (EA). These encounters were likely to take place very suddenly and be over very quickly. Usually they would take place at section level (4 to 8 men). EA drills were to be extensively taught and practised. The principles were simplicity, aggression, speed and flexibility.

There were three types of encounters: initiative with SF (terrorists seen first), initiative with both sides (simultaneous sighting) and initiative with the terrorists (ambush or fired upon).

In the first type of EA, leading elements give silent signals, all go to ground, close in and open fire on terrorists when in the best killing ground. Then reorganize. In the second and third types of EA, elements in contact would go to ground in cover and skirmish to consolidate, using the well-practised fire and movement, and assault. Then reorganize. This type of encounter was very much like the section battle drills of the classical warfare.

Reorganization would entail taking up a position of all-round defence, sending a contact report, attending to own casualties, carrying out a thorough clearance of the area, securing live terrorists, making sure dead ones were really dead, selecting a LZ for helicopters for casevac and deploying extra troops and organising a follow up.

After lunch there was a short lecture on contact reports. These were delivered by radio to one's base. They started with the words "Contact, contact, contact." Then followed the grid reference of the contact given in clear, it was never to be sent in code, terrorist strength, SF casualties, terrorist casualties and any other information that was relevant. We took turns at making some up and delivering them.

After supper we went along with virtually the whole of the School of Infantry personnel to 132's initiation concert in the National Service Officer Cadet Mess. It seemed a fleeting moment since we had performed there ourselves.

It was a great show, I thought, better than ours. The highlights for me were Pete Arnold, attired in full dinner jacket, reciting from memory the whole of "Eskimo Nell" in a plum English accent with a totally straight face, and a comedy take on "Goldilocks and the Three Bears". Daddy Bear was replaced by Hallamore Bear taking off Sergeant Major Hallamore. One of his lines was a reminder of his obsession with ankle puttees. "The left hand side of this porridge is a clear half-inch above the right hand side! You're on a charge!"

Yet again, we partied on into the small hours, but without the aid of fire extinguishers this time.

Thursday 19 July

We started the day with foot-drill revision. We hadn't been on the Drill Square for some time and so were a little rusty but it all soon came back to us. Colour Wales didn't overdo it and it was all a lot less painful than we had anticipated.

The first lecture of the morning was on convoys and convoy orders, to be followed by one on anti-ambush drills. Essentially there were two types of convoy, purely military convoys and combined civilian/military convoys with the military providing the protection. First priority would be to get a convoy through, and this object was never to be compromised.

When giving orders one had to cover the destination, the composition of the convoy and the situation with regard to possible enemy forces (as the war progressed convoys were ambushed more and more) and their likely location along the road.

Then came the more minute detail such as the order of march with the exact position of military vehicles, if it was a civilian/military convoy, and their level of armament.

Other detail would include the convoy speed, the exact route, the vehicle separation (this would vary according to terrain), the exact sites for smoke breaks if needed and the procedure for all-round defence during smoke breaks.

One would have to consider what to do if there was a breakdown (basically here the vehicle would be abandoned and the drivers/passengers taken up by the first following military vehicle) and designate places for refuelling.

The action to be taken in the event of an ambush would have to be stipulated (vehicles were to drive straight on unless disabled, in which case the military would proceed with anti-ambush drills).

For the military the usual checks of rations, water,

ammunition, weapons, radio communications and other equipment would be done.

Throughout the orders there would be a constant reminder of convoy discipline, namely maintenance of order of march, speed and dispersion of the convoy.

We moved onto anti-ambush drills. Methods of de-bussing were covered and after that one proceeded as with any encounter action.

A favourite with the DS was the method of debussing off the back of vehicles while they were still moving. You had to leap out to counter the speed of the vehicle so as to compensate for it and keep your footing on landing. Easier in theory than in practice, as we were to find out!

After lunch we had another administration lecture from Staff Sergeant Pearce. He assured us all that what we were about to learn would be easy.

We spent the time filling out the various forms for issue and receipt of rations with fictitious orders, all done at the Platoon Commander level. We took on the role of issuer and receiver in each case. We compiled RA/Q/34 forms to get rations from the CQMS, RA/Q/51 forms for issue on detachment and Z828T forms to draw rations from civilian suppliers. At one stage I took the part of a harassed African bush store manager who was not too keen on accepting a Z828T form instead of cash!

At the end of the lecture Staff Pearce seemed quite pleased with results.

The last lecture of the day was on sweeps. Sweeps were designed to flush out terrorists, but could be very difficult to control, especially in thick bush.

A successful sweep relied on good security; it was no use if the terrorists knew it was coming. It was also necessary to have sufficient troops for the task and good control had to be kept, involving excellent communications and a rate of advance slow enough to ensure thorough search of the ground.

Three groups were involved in a sweep – stop groups, the sweep party and the reserve party. The sweep party would ideally consist of two lines of sub-units, one 200m in front of the other. Report lines would have to be used and no sub-units were to advance until all units had reached these lines. FNs or shot guns were the preferred weapons for sweep parties.

Stop groups were generally a section of four men with one MAG and three FNs to supply a high rate of fire. These were designed to stop any terrorists who had eluded the sweep party or were running from them.

Stop groups had to be placed on three sides of the area to be swept. They had to move quietly into position using cover and were to detain any people encountered on the way in. On arrival of the sweeping sub-units the stop group was to stand up and give the recognition signal.

The reserve party was there to help engage any found terrorists and to carry out any necessary follow-ups.

Friday 20 July

The morning was spent on Administration. We first covered the issuing and receipt of clothing, expendables such as radio batteries and accommodation stores such as stretchers. At the Platoon Commander level the ubiquitous RA/Q/1033 form was used.

We then moved onto the very strictly controlled indenting and accounting for ammunition, explosives, controlled items such as compasses and radios and weapons.

All controlled items and weapons would be initially signed for by the Platoon Commander, recorded in the controlled stores book, RA/Q/183, and then issued to and signed for by the troops individually. During deployment constant checks of possession and serial numbers would have to be made. It was recommended that quantity should be checked daily and the serial numbers checked weekly.

Training and first-line ammunition, grenades and pyrotechnics were indented for by and issued by the unit CSM and accounted for by declaration certificates or contact reports signed by the Platoon Commander.

Obviously there was a great deal of trust put in the hands of the Platoon Commander. Staff Sergeant Pearce told us of the case when in the field, on the shores of Lake Kariba, a certain Platoon Commander accounted for three HE grenades being used by declaring that they had deep cracks in their casings and had to be detonated. It turned out that they had been used to kill fish in the lake to feed the platoon.

The last part of the morning was spent on MT (Motor Transport) accounting and focused on the vehicle log book, the RA/Q/23.

It was designed to last about two years and was used to show that the vehicle's use was authorized by signature. Only an officer could do this. It was also used to record refuelling from military fuelling points, with the quantity of fuel issued and the date of refueling being recorded. Fuel was signed for by the driver and recorded in the log book by the bowser operator.

Records of repairs, servicing and transfer of vehicle to other units were also entered in the log book. The log book was a very important document, often supplying evidence in Boards of Inquiry, and its loss would be taken very seriously.

After lunch was a fitness test, consisting of a ten-mile march along the Gwelo-Bulawayo Road in full battle dress. We all came through this well and were rewarded with a weekend pass. It wasn't all that great for me as I had to play rugby on the Sunday, but I had decided to have at least Friday and Saturday nights in Salisbury. I had tickets for the Vienna Boys' Choir on Saturday.

I enjoyed the trip to Salisbury with Mike Lambiris and Pete Arnold from Intake 132 for company. In particular we discussed a bloke on their course who showed overwhelming confidence in his ability. We debated if it was real or just put on to impress and wondered if, as a result, he was likely to be commissioned.

Ultimately, we all thought that nineteen weeks of close scrutiny by our instructors during the course would settle the thing one way or another.

Bill Cock had very kindly offered to put me up for the Friday and Saturday nights. I arrived in time for a dinner party at Bill's place with Ann Posner and Alec and Dawn Siemers. It was a great evening and fascinating to hear their anecdotes of Prince Edward in the fifties and the characters of the times.

Saturday 21 July

Breakfast with Bill and then off to Borrowdale to see the folks. I got a bombshell when I arrived. Jock, the family pet, an Alsatian, had died the previous evening of suspected poisoning.

My father in particular was quite upset. We immediately went out after reading an advert in the newspaper and were luckily able to buy another Alsatian, this time a female.

In the evening I took my mother to see the Vienna Boys' Choir, something she had wanted to do all her life, at the Harry Margolis Hall.

Sunday 22 July

I left for Gwelo at 0800hrs and got in at 1130hrs. A leisurely lunch at School of Infantry was followed by a drive to Shabani for the rugby game.

The game was quite rough, these miners were hard men. My opposite number was sent off for shoulder-barging me. A little unfair, as I was perfectly all right, but the referee was boss.

I managed to score a try with a desperate lunge for the corner but in the process must have done something to my left shoulder. I didn't feel anything at the time but after showers I felt a pain which gradually got worse as the evening wore on, despite several after-hostilities beers. During the night I found I could only lie on my back or right side.

Monday 23 July

For the first time I dodged a parade to visit the MI room. Luckily for me it was the dreaded musters. I certainly couldn't swing my arm. I had a torn ligament, to which liniment would have to be applied.

I got to our lecture room just in time for the first morning session. The topic was cordon and search, carried out mostly to find terrorists and weapons. We had touched briefly on this when we had our day with the BSAP and indeed Lieutenant McDermott emphasized right from the outset that for cordon and search operations the Army and BSAP would combine.

Several separate parties were needed for a successful cordon and search. They were cordon troops, outer cordon troops, search teams, cage troops, screen teams, escort troops and road block troops. With the exception of a few BSAP personnel for the search teams and screen teams, the Army would provide most of the personnel for these parties.

The BSAP decided on the area to be searched, carried out a plain clothes recce and warned inhabitants once the cordon was in place. Depending on the scale and importance of the cordon and search, the Air Force could be called upon to provide aerial OP.

The aim was to surround the area as quickly as possible. To facilitate this, cordon troops should approach from as many directions as possible. The establishment of the cordon was to be communicated to the cordoned population through their leader, or with the use of a loudspeaker or banner. People could be confined to their houses by means of a curfew or, in the case of a small village, all moved to a central point.

The central point should be established in any case, sited in shade on clean stone-free ground with areas cordoned off to house unscreened males, unscreened females, screened males, screened females, wanted/suspected males and wanted/suspected females.

Once the search was over, all people who had been screened would be released. The wanted/suspected people would be taken to the local police station for further investigation. Escort troops would assist in transporting them there.

Searchers would then move in, escorted by troops. Each search party would need to have at least one woman member for the searching of female suspects.

When a house was to be searched, if people were in the building they should be moved to one room for preliminary screening, which might or might not involve a search, and then be kept there.

Each room should be searched from top to bottom. When checking the floor for possible buried weapons or explosives, if it was a dirt floor, a proved method of detection was to pour water on the floor and watch for any obviously more rapid draining indicating disturbed earth. A metal detector was also very useful.

Once the house had been searched the occupants would be moved to the central point for further searching and/or questioning. If possible, it was preferable to leave one person in the house to avoid looting. It was also necessary to get the head of the house to sign a paper saying that no thieving took place during the search. The cordon would then be closed in to avoid a house being searched twice.

Lieutenant McDermott emphasized the importance of not breaking into a house except in the case of absence of occupants or resistance. Also he emphasized the danger of being accused of theft by the occupants.

After lunch we had a cloth model and went through the whole process of cordon and search again. We covered both large-scale and small-scale searches.

In the evening we all met in our mess for a farewell to Billy Green. He was being invalided out of the Army because of a groin injury that could not heal quickly and prevented him from taking part in any physical activity. We all went down to Gwelo station to see him off. With only four weeks to go it was a shame to see him leave. He was a cheerful soul to have about the place, even after mercilessly being given the dubious sobriquet of "Billy Groin".

Tuesday 24 July

The morning was spent learning about urban drills, basically crowd control and/or crowd dispersion.

Lieutenant McDermott mentioned that most Army people dreaded the thought of carrying out a crowd-dispersion and emphasized that the overriding principle of minimum use of force was to be born in mind.

Urban drills were normally the province of the BSAP, but the military could be called on to take over by a District Commissioner, a Magistrate or the Police if they felt that they could not cope with the situation. It would be up to the military commander at whatever level to agree or refuse to take over.

There were three phases with urban drills, the standby phase, the passive phase and the active phase.

During the standby phase a W FOL 6 form, authorizing the military to take over, had to be filled in by all parties concerned. While this was being done troops would be made ready, transport arranged and orders given.

The passive phase covered the actual deployment of troops to the area and moving in on foot in patrol formation before adopting riot formation. We covered these formations in detail, at both platoon and company levels, with regard to positioning of the MAG gunners and riflemen and firing positions adopted, kneeling or standing.

The movement in on foot was to be disciplined, very smart, as on a drill square, and words of command were to be kept to a minimum. Rifles would be at the high port. A recorder should accompany the formation to make a note of every move or decision made. A radio operator and stretcher bearers would also accompany the formations.

The active phase covered the actual drill for dispersing the crowd. After adopting riot formation the crowd would be told to disperse and given time to do so. If they did not and appeared to become more threatening, it would be up to the military commander to order one particular soldier to open fire on a picked individual with one round.

Further orders to open fire could be issued if the crowd still did not disperse. The 2IC of the unit would then pick up any empty cartridge cases. Bodies or wounded were then to be collected by stretcher bearers. Control would finally be handed over to the civil authorities.

As could be expected quite a few questions were fired at Lieutenant McDermott. One obvious one was why warning shots would not be fired. We were told that after the incident in

Nyasaland in the late fifties when warning shots were fired without any crowd dispersal resulting, it had been decided that we would show that we "meant business" when we actually opened fire on one individual. At the end of this session we could see why one would dread carrying out urban drills.

Before lunch we were shown a film about urban drills called "Keeping the Peace".

The afternoon was spent preparing for and collecting non-perishable stores for our COIN battle camp to take place in the Selukwe area from Wednesday to Friday. We were to cover the establishment of platoon and patrol bases, patrolling, EA drills, vehicle anti-ambush drills and ambushes.

Wednesday 25 July

We collected perishable rations from the mess kitchen and weapons, ammunition, grenades and flares from the armoury, then loaded up the RL and headed off for the Selukwe area.

We spent the afternoon moving into our base camp, sited by Lieutenant McDermott. We were then left alone completely to set everything up. We dug shell-scrapes and put up camouflaged bivvies (steeply pitched shelters using waterproof sheets). We were on this exercise with African demonstration troops seconded from the RAR.

Rob Mutch was appointed as "Platoon Commander" and sent me, as one of the appointed "Sergeants", on a 360 patrol in charge of a section of three demonstration troops.

This had to be done quietly, using silent signals. We had practised moving with silent signals but this was the first time that I had done this with experienced troops. Amazingly to me, it all went perfectly, with them totally understanding my signals and responding immediately as required. It was definitely a sound testament to our training.

During the afternoon while we were setting up the base I had a chance to talk to some of the demonstration troops who were with us but not required to dig shellscrapes or camouflage their bivvies. One of them turned out to be from the area of Ngomokurira near Domboshawa where I had done a bit of walking as a schoolboy. When I suggested that he must be disappointed about being on this exercise and stationed at Gwelo instead of being operational with the RAR, he laughed.

"No" he said, "I am glad. I will not be killed. I am in the Army because I need the money."

He had been amazingly honest, and I wondered how many other Africans were in the same boat and felt the same way.

In the early evening Colour Wales came to our position and told us that we were now "untac" and took us across to the DS camp for a supper at trestle tables with George the waiter to wash up. So this was how the other half lived. The DS lived in the lap of luxury while we trainees grubbed around in trenches or shellscrapes; nice of them to share it with us even for a short time!

During the supper I struck up a conversation with Hayden Whisken, who was with us on the exercise as a medic. He told me that over the Rhodes and Founders weekend his girlfriend had been killed in a car crash. This was terrible news. I offered my condolences of course, but felt as I suppose one always does on these occasions that words were useless.

Still at the DS camp we had a lecture on the heavy barrel FN and the semi-automatic shotgun, before wending our way back to our bivvies.

Thursday 26 July

Breakfast was also at the DS camp; things seemed to be looking up. We then walked up a vlei valley (a grass-covered valley with clay soils, easily flooded) in full weapon training order to practise helicopter drills. We selected a suitable LZ and waited in sticks of four to be picked up by choppers for a quick circuit and then to be dropped off with it hovering about four feet off the ground.

Most of us had never been in a helicopter before and we were surprised at the wind it generated as it came closer to the ground. We had been told to remove our camouflage caps to avoid them being blown off our heads. We were also surprised at how safe we felt in the chopper – it seemed there was no chance of falling out, despite not having any seat belts. It was all down to centripetal force.

There was a quick change of appointments. I was made "Platoon Commander" and we moved onto vehicle anti-ambush drills. For a couple of hours we practised these. We rode in the RL until we heard an explosion (thunder-flashes set off by Colour Wales moving ahead in a Land Rover). We would then jump out and attack an imaginary enemy position, manned by Colour Wales and a few demonstration troops.

As taught, we would go to ground and fire at cover or smoke from small arms fire, skirmish to consolidate and assault. We would then take up a position of all-round defence, sweep the area, secure the enemy and send a contact report.

By the end of this time we were tired out, but it was all becoming second nature. We were given ration packs and sent back to our base for lunch.

After lunch, as the new "Platoon Commander", I was called to the radio. "Come to the Company HQ in five minutes, we have received some interesting information."

It was Lieutenant McDermott's voice taking the role of "Company Commander". I assumed Company HQ was the DS camp, and off I went playing my role as "Platoon Commander".

I often felt on these occasions that I would have been better at playing soldiers when I was ten years old than now, but I realized that this was probably the only way we could train for the job ahead. I never really got the hang of it.

I was given information that "gooks" were coming to the waterhole that we had passed on our way to the helicopter drills that morning and that we were to ambush them. We were to be in position by 2000 hours. Armed with this intelligence, I went back to the base to prepare my orders.

I did a quick time appreciation and felt that I had the time to do a quick recce of the ambush position, prepare and give orders and then squeeze in a daylight rehearsal before sunset. I was about to take a section out to do the recce when Lieutenant McDermott and Colour Wales arrived. They told us that they were unimpressed with our bivvies and would get some demonstration troops to show us how to set up a properly-camouflaged one.

We watched while they did this. We had to admit theirs was better than ours, but by the time they had finished it was too late for a recce or a daylight rehearsal. So much for Lieutenant McDermott's time appreciation, allowing subordinates time to plan.

In fact it was almost too late for me to prepare orders, but I managed to throw something together with a model based on the 1:50,000 map, and started to deliver the orders just before we lost the light.

As mentioned before, ambush orders are incredibly complex. There is so much to be covered and it took me about twenty minutes to deliver them. Dusk was almost on us before I had finished.

I felt that they had gone all right, but I was still amazed when there was no comment from Lieutenant McDermott about its delivery. Either it was OK or it was so bad he had given up on me.

We had a night rehearsal in the area of the base, covering

order of march, section dropping-off points, warning the whole unit of the approach of terrs towards the ambush position and initiating the ambush.

The warning of approach was to be given by the first section to sight or hear the terrs. It was done by holding down the prestle switch of a radio, on very low volume, for about two seconds. This would cause an interruption of the static.

After a final inspection of equipment we set off for the position at 1900 hours. My section, due to occupy the ambush position, led the way along the path up the vlei valley. I could then drop off the sections in the correct sequence and in the correct areas, drop my section off in our position and guide the last few sections past my position and then return.

In the killing area we quickly set up a trip flare with the wire leading to our position. The setting off of this flare would initiate the ambush and give us light to see by. It was overcast and very dark. We were all in position by 1945 hours. I was quite pleased with myself, believing that it had all gone well so far and relaxed. It was simply a case of waiting to spring the ambush.

We waited and waited; 2000 hours, 2015 hours, 2030 hours and nothing. It was very cold. I temporarily closed my eyes.

I awoke with a jerk to look at my luminous watch. It was 2200 hours. There was still no sign of the "terrs". 2230 hours, 2300 hours and slowly it dawned on me. I had been asleep and missed the ambush. So had the rest of my section, and so had most of the rest of the platoon. We lay there freezing until dawn.

Friday 27 July

With daylight came a shout. "Close in!" It was Lieutenant McDermott. We all left our positions and closed around him for a de-briefing.

We all copped a massive "rev". The DS, who had been playing the part of the "terrs", were totally unimpressed. We were told that we were useless. They told us that as they walked along the path they heard snoring. At the waterhole they had even thrown a stone into the water to try to alert us. They then walked away and decided to leave us in position all night as a punishment for missing the ambush.

While the whole debacle was not just my fault I certainly felt that I had totally messed up and that I was more culpable than anyone else. One section had given a warning of the approach of the "enemy" by holding down the prestle switch on their radio, but I had not heard this. I felt even worse when the DS failed to point my failure out. I'm sure they must have guessed that I had been asleep at the crucial moment, but apart from the general accusation about the snoring nothing was said.

I also reflected on the fact that sleeping on guard when on active service was a serious offence. I suppose in training things could be different. I still expected some sort of retribution.

Without any breakfast, we began an imaginary follow-up. The demonstration troops from the ambush were allowed to return to the base.

We set off without any breakfast at 0630 hours. We moved up the vlei valley, which soon became steeper and rockier with kopjes and outcrops. We were fired upon by "terrs" (Colour Wales and some other demonstration troops) and again carried out EA drills including the time-worn fire and movement. Each time we completed these, as had happened in the vehicle anti-ambush drills yesterday, Colour Wales and the other "terrs" would miraculously come to life and move off up the valley. We had to wait a few minutes before setting off again towards another "ambush".

Although this was all becoming second nature, there were still lessons to be learnt. At the end of one drill we were in the re-organisation stage and Colour Wales was "dead" on the ground holding an FN. I grabbed his rifle by the muzzle-guard to remove it and he squeezed the trigger. It was firing blanks, but the flash from the discharge came right through the muzzle-guard and burnt my hand. I was fairly fed up and resolved the next time to kick him hard in the ribs to make sure that he was "dead", adding my own touch of realism to the situation. The exercise ended before I could do this. Probably just as well, as I could have been charged with assaulting a superior!

By the end, at 1100 hours, we were totally drained. We were taken by RL back to our camp and told to re-do our bivvies as we had been shown the previous evening. The DS seemed satisfied with our efforts. We were given a lunch at the DS camp.

The remaining demonstration troops departed for the

School of Infantry and our course stayed. Lieutenant McDermott called us together.

"We have some good news and some bad news", he said. "First the good news; because your little ambush yesterday was so bad, we'll let you do another one tonight. The bad news is that after the ambush you can make your own way back to Gwelo."

We went white, but then realized that he was only joking.

"No", he said "the good news is that we are going home tonight."

The first part of the afternoon was spent throwing M962 Mills grenades. These required a fuse to be screwed in before they could be used. They had a seven-second delay. We took turns in throwing them from a dug-out. We would screw in the fuse, pull the pin and throw the grenade, then watch it and count to five before ducking down just before the explosion.

Lieutenant McDermott then demonstrated the throwing of a white phosphorus grenade. This was a particularly vicious piece of ordinance. It did not have to be primed, needing only the pulling of the pin and the release of the handle to operate. It had a four-second delay. On exploding it would spray a circle of white phosphorus liquid out to a radius of about thirty feet with an all-round trajectory of white smoke. All this white phosphorus would then burn intensely for quite a while.

It could be used to create a smoke marker, but its main use was to flush enemy out of cover. Just a drop of white phosphorus on one's skin would result in severe burns as until it was used up, the only way of extinguishing it was total immersion in water.

Lieutenant McDermott got us in a circle of about fifty feet in radius in an area of grassland. As a precaution we had used our pangas to cut green branches ready to do a spot of fire-fighting.

He then threw the grenade into the middle of this circle. We attacked the flames just outside the circle of white phosphorus so that we didn't pick up any and cause the fire to spread. It was all unfortunately to no avail. The grass was too dry and just too long and, with a bit of wind, the fire got out of control.

We battled it for about ten minutes, with the situation getting worse and the fire spreading, when the farmer whose land we were on arrived in a Land Rover ahead of a tractor with a trailer carrying his workforce of about twenty labourers. With their help we finally got the fire under control.

The farmer seemed to take it all in his stride, but a grateful Lieutenant McDermott made him a present of several hundred rounds for his FN by way of compensation for burning quite a few acres of his land. He was lucky the whole farm didn't go up in smoke.

It was nice to know that Lieutenant McDermott could also make "cock-ups" occasionally.

We regrouped on a hill to wait to commence the last bit of our training for the afternoon. We were very thirsty and were allowed to rest, drinking copiously from our water bottles. John Richardson mumbled something about "fire and movement" and got a laugh, even from the DS.

We then practised sharpshooting with the automatic shotgun. In thicker bush, when a target presented itself, it was necessary to shoot at it in the shortest possible time. This did not allow for an aimed shot. The weapon had to be considered an extension of the arm.

We took turns to walk a path, opening fire, with live shells, on targets that came into sight as we walked along. The spray of the shot made for an almost certain hit each time.

We took off for Gwelo and got back at about 1900 hours. We parked the RL with weapons and stores in a lock-up garage in the armoury enclosure, then changed and went into town to a café for a hamburger before falling into a welcome bed.

Saturday 28 July

After breakfast we handed in stores and weapons, then Digby Neuhoff and I took off for Salisbury. There was to be no more rugby for me for the rest of the course because of the shoulder injury.

Rex McCulloch had kindly fixed up a bed for me on the resident master's veranda at Rhodes House at Prince Edward for the weekend. We went down to the Europa Café for lunch after a couple of beers at the Jameson House pub and then on to watch the rugby matches on Jubilee Field against Alan Wilson.

After the games the staff from both schools went for drinks at Ray Suttle's house on the school grounds. Ray was the headmaster of Prince Edward. Then Piet de Bruin, Rex McCullough and I went to Demi's restaurant, opposite the State Lottery Hall, before finishing off in the Jameson House pub for a nightcap.

Sunday 29 July

I was up fairly early and off to spend the day and have lunch with friends Peter and Heather Waddell on their farm out at Mazoe. Their son Colin and his friend Kevin Cookson were at home for the weekend, both on leave from Selous House at Prince Edward, and I was able to give them a lift back in the afternoon to save Peter the drive to return them to school.

The Waddells had a small dog called Rusty. As mentioned, this happened to be my nickname amongst the boys at Prince Edward. Colin and Kevin had the greatest delight calling the dog to them, "Come on Rusty. Have a dog biscuit!" all the while smiling at me to see my reaction.

Sadly Kevin was killed a few years later in a hunting accident. His older brother Doug Cookson, also a Selous House boy, died in action with the RLI on 28 February 1976.

At Prince Edward I visited Peter and Glen Kolbe, attended the service at the school chapel and had a drink with Bill Cock before picking up Digby Neuhoff at the Jameson Hotel for our drive back to Gwelo via Umvuma. It had been a great weekend.

Monday 30 July

There was a scheduled three-hour session on the revision of Q accounting and M.T. accounting, followed by Static POL accounting. Staff Sergeant Pearce covered it all in one hour. His technique was to inspire confidence by repeatedly saying, at the end of each topic, "Easy, piece of piss. We know that now."

His lectures were always short, sharp and to the point. This made a pleasant change from what we were used to – we often thought that lectures, cloth model sessions and 'tewts' went on too long.

Static POL accounting covered the drawing of a bowser full of fuel on the 1033 and running one's own 825 when issuing fuel. A bowser of fuel could only be drawn with written authority from the company commander. Again, although we did not see all this military accounting as vitally important in our training, it was amazing how much of it was used when we did eventually go operational.

After Staff Sergeant Pearce dismissed us early we went to the mess and killed time until Lieutenant McDermott's lecture at 1110 hours. The lecture was on attacks on a terr hide. Information about the position of a terr hide was usually gleaned from a captured terr. Finding the exact position could be difficult, as terrs could not always map read. An African interpreter familiar with the area was often used to help locate it.

It should be expected that terrs would oppose any attack

strongly from prepared positions. Sentries would be alert and would give the alarm. On SF being seen they could fire a round, run into camp or use bird or animal calls as a warning.

The composition of the attacking force would be as follows. A command group which would be small, consisting of the commander, a radio operator and a medic, would be positioned to control the actual attack. It could be airborne.

Stop groups, in sticks of five with MAG and radio, would cover all likely escape routes from the terr camp, be concealed, would know the position of nearby groups and stay in position until told to move.

A fire group would approach as near to the camp as possible and support the assault group with maximum fire.

The assault group would skirmish forward and physically clear the camp. It would then split into two, one half to search the camp for POWs and weapons and the other half to do a 360 for tracks, after alerting the stop groups by radio. The stop groups could also side-step to look for tracks.

Follow up groups would pick up any discovered tracks. There would also be a reserve nearby for reinforcements. Depending on the scale of the attack, support or initial bombardment could be given by mortars, artillery and aircraft. Helicopters could be standing by for evacuating casualties and captured terrs.

As a portent of things to come we were given a set of safety distances for various bombs and projectiles. These were for

81mm mortar shells - 100 yards, 25lb artillery shells - 150 yards, 250lb bomb - 400 yards, 500lb bomb - 750 yards, 1000lb bomb - 1000 yards and 50lb fran-tan bomb 100 yards.

During the war many attacks were made on terr hides or camps, the most affective of which were probably the attacks on Chimoio and Mapai in Mozambique in 1979, named Operation Dingo and Operation Miracle respectively. Both were initiated by an aerial bombardment. It was estimated that 3000 terrs were killed for the loss of two security force personnel at Chimoio and 300 terrs for the loss of 15 security force personnel at Mapai. One was another Prince Edward old boy, Gert O'Niell, killed in action on 27 September 1979.

The afternoon was spent having a session, largely in the form of a discussion, on leadership, man-management and morale. We were encouraged to speak freely on these topics and on our own experience in the Army so far. Some of our ideas did not at all coincide with those of Lieutenant McDermott and Colour Wales, but they listened to each of us in turn before vouchsafing their own opinions.

We were coming from the standpoint of having to deal in the future with men whose outlook, even when on call-up, would be essentially civilian. We felt that too much in the way of excessive "revving" would be counter-productive for leadership, man-management and morale.

I mentioned the incident during our defensive exercise when Keith Lindsay misread his withdrawal route and the way in which the "rev" that he had received was in my opinion too prolonged. I also mentioned the "rev" that I had received from Lieutenant McDermott when I had used the word "please" when telling someone on my course to stack ammunition on the range.

They countered with a cautionary note on making sure we did not let our troops see us as weak and start taking advantage of us. Colour Wales did agree with us to a certain extent, to the point of saying that we and many of the men we would command would never be "real soldiers" but told us that firm discipline was necessary nevertheless.

That evening John Richardson and I had an excellent dinner at the Midlands Hotel, followed by a few drinks at the Traveler's Retreat before bed.

Unfortunately five from our course were again on guard duty, John and I luckily being on the roster for the next guard duty. That wouldn't be too far in the future, we were sure.

Tuesday 31 July

During the morning we had a tewt on attacking a terr hide.

We went into the training area at the School of Infantry. We were given a briefing on the reported existence of a terr hide with a position and briefed on our supposed strength to carry out the attack.

This time it was Pete Nupen who had to give the orders. As

usual, unless we were on an exercise and had appointments, we all had to prepare them but only one of us delivered the orders. Then we went through the process of the attack without weapons, some of us simulating an attack group, some a fire group and the rest of us stop groups. We had to simulate, by walking through, moving into position, attacking and afterwards searching for tracks.

The morning ended with a short debrief. The main criticism was the noise we made moving into position. Luckily we were not so bad that we had to do it again.

Just before we went off to lunch we were told out of the blue that we would be moving from the Montgomery barrack room to rooms in the Regular Officer Cadets' Mess as soon as our afternoon's lecture was over. No reason for the move was given but we certainly didn't object. We would without doubt be moving up in the luxury stakes.

After lunch we had our last MT administration lecture from "Piss-easy" Pearce, as he was now affectionately known. It was a very short lecture on accident reports and filling out an RA/Q/406 form. We spent the rest of the afternoon making the move to our new quarters.

The Regular Officer Cadets' Mess was like a hotel - two to a room, carpets in the corridors, showers in the building and wash basins in our rooms. We would still have to eat our meals and drink in the NS Officer Cadets' Mess. I would be sharing a room with Pete Nupen.

In the evening some of us managed a little bit of study for the up-coming final exams on Thursday 9 August before abandoning the library for the mess.

It was interesting to note that everybody's alcohol consumption had gone up since the start of second phase. Certainly a few drinks in the mess relaxed us all after the daily grind.

Wednesday 1 August

The first lecture of the morning was a recap of our lecture, in early July, on GAC procedure. We were told that we would be practising this on Friday at Kutanga with Provosts to guide in to imaginary targets. To add to what we had been told before, we were given the call signs of all the various squadrons to use with GAC.

This was followed by a lecture on LZs and DZs, landing zones and dropping zones. A DZ was a specified area on which troops, supplies and equipment would be dropped by parachute. Ideally a DZ and surrounding areas would be close to ground troops and clear of obstacles, with the grass cover as short as possible to avoid loss. It should be easily located from the air, with the approach and departure routes free of enemy forces. If possible the approach should not be into the sun, although this would depend on wind direction.

The pilot would have to be notified by radio of the grid

reference of the impact point, the magnetic bearing of the axis of the DZ and approach and the wind speed and direction.

The DZ should be about 200 yards wide and 500 yards long and the long side should be in the direction of the wind.

The plane would approach, at 500 feet (1000 feet at night) downwind of the DZ at right angles to the wind direction and release parachutes above an aiming point selected by troops on the ground and signalled by flare (a torch would suffice at night). It would be used or not used at the discretion of the pilot.

To assist the ground forces in selecting a suitable aiming point, one could expect a parachute to drift 70 yards in falling 500 feet for every 5 mph of wind speed.

An "A" formed with rectangular day-glow panels with a horizontal strip underneath would signal "clear to drop", whereas an "A" with a cross underneath would signal "drop cancelled".

LZs were places where helicopters could alight. Any fixed wing aircraft LZs would be constructed by the Air Force. LZs would have to be circular, with an inner ring of 15 yards diameter with grass down to ground level and a concentric outer ring of diameter of 50 yards where the grass could not be above four feet in height. It might be necessary to cut the grass to meet these requirements.

Hard standing was obligatory. We were reminded that in our helicopter training on our battle camp, the chopper had landed on a dry vlei.

At night the dimensions of the LZ were to be doubled linearly and lit with vehicle headlights or a "T" formed of five lights or flares approximately 10 yards apart with the horizontal bar upwind at right angles to the wind direction and on the edge of the inner circle. The vertical bar of the "T" would also be at the edge of the inner circle.

The first part of the afternoon was spent on a lecture about pistol firing. We would be firing 32mm pistols with a magazine of eight rounds.

The rest of the afternoon was spent on the short range, learning about firing positions and one-handed and two-handed discharging. We then took turns to practise live firing. In all, we each fired off four magazines.

At the end of this session we were given the glad tidings that we were again on guard duty. Would it ever end?

Thursday 2 August

The morning was spent covering the follow-up. This could occur if tracks were found, but normally after a contact. A trained tracker would have to be included in the follow-up group.

We asked Lieutenant McDermott if we would have any training in tracking ourselves before the end of the course. He told us that time prevented this, as to learn anything worthwhile much more time would be needed. He cited the beginners' tracking course run by Combat Tracker Unit at Kariba, which lasted three weeks.

During follow-ups SF could be required to travel long distances over several days with very little rest. Ideally follow-up troops should be replaced after 48 hours, but this was not always possible. With an enhanced chance of contact, there was a minimum scale of equipment to carry.

Each rifleman would carry webbing, 150 rounds of ball in five magazines of 20 rounds each (tracer should be included in each magazine) and a bandolier of 50 rounds (also interspaced with tracer), one HE grenade, one white phosphorus grenade, one anti-personnel rifle grenade, a flare, a bed roll, a panga, at least two water bottles and kidney pouches containing three days' rations, water sterilizing tablets, a rifle cleaning kit, mosquito repellant, a face veil and a first field dressing.

Each machine gunner would carry everything above except that it would be 350 rounds of ball in belts instead of the 150 rounds carried by a rifleman.

The follow-up commander would carry all that a rifleman did plus a mini flare projector, with ten flares and a smoke grenade to indicate FLOT when using GAC.

The commander and second in command and each section should also carry a dog whistle, relevant maps, compass, protractor and note-book and pencil.

Each section and the follow up commander's party should carry a VHF radio, spare batteries, a unit scant list and slidex cards and a J-Pack. A J-Pack was a medical pack containing a snake bite outfit, morphine in ampoules, various dressings and bandages, pain killing tablets, antiseptic, suturing equipment, penicillin and syringes.

We learned that most success in follow-ups occurred when contacts took place earlier on in the day and when unexpected by the terrs.

In the afternoon we once again practised EA drills, but this time we were made to negotiate the assault course several times in the process with Colour Wales having a high old time letting off thunder flashes in front of and to the side of us as we moved along. During the process I twisted by shoulder again and battled to finish the exercise.

It was good to go early to bed.

Friday 3 August

We were up at 0530 hours for an early cereal breakfast and then on the road to Kutanga. We spent all morning rehearsing GAC procedure on the radio before each of us took turns to guide provosts in on a target using smoke grenades to indicate FLOT.

We were very impressed with the Air Force and how well they coped with our rankly amateurish efforts. The actual experience of calling in aircraft successfully was quite edifying, leaving us feeling that at last we were getting the idea of command and control.

After another luxury lunch, Air Force style, we moved onto firing the 60mm mortar. This weapon had replaced the old two-inch mortar with which we had become acquainted earlier on in our training. It consisted of a smoothbore metal tube on a rectangular base plate. It was supported by a bipod with sights for elevating and traversing. The firing pin was fixed at the base of the tube allowing the mortar bomb to fire on being dropped down the barrel. The two-inch mortar had a trigger mechanism.

The weight of the 60mm mortar was 19 kg with an HE bomb of 1.3 kg. It fired with an elevation from 40 degrees to 85 degrees and could traverse 8 degrees.

Maximum rate of fire, because of the fixed firing pin, was 18 rounds per minute. The muzzle velocity was 518 feet per second and its maximum range was 1800 yards.

We each had a turn at setting the mortar and dropping the bomb in the tube, once again with some success. It was all direct fire, which meant we could line up the target when traversing. Elevation would come with experience.

This weapon had an indirect firing capability, but this was beyond our level of training.

We then fired the MAG on a tripod for the first time before being given a demolition demonstration much along the lines of that at the School of Military Engineering in Bulawayo.

Some of us had decided not to take weekend leave and those that stayed had a few quiet drinks in the mess before an early bed.

Saturday 4 August

Charlie Lenegan and I had a leisurely morning in Gwelo buying a few mundane things and having tea and toast at Marche's Restaurant. We studied in the afternoon in preparation for our final academic and practical exams, due to be taken on Thursday and Friday the next week.

The evening was spent on a mini pub-crawl around Gwelo. At some stage Sel Stevens joined us and we finished up at the Gwelo Sports Club. We hit our beds at about midnight.

Sunday 5 August

Feeling a little under the weather we mooched about the camp for the morning getting in a bit more studying, but after lunch a small group of us went and had a round of golf at Selukwe.

After the excesses of the previous night the idea had been to have quiet evening. It wasn't to be. We got back to the School of Infantry, after a meal at the Midlands Hotel, intending to have a quick night cap before bed. We entered our mess to find a group of men, most of whom we didn't recognize, dressed in civvies, although, from their bearing and the fact that they were with Captain Dawson from tactical wing, we could see they were obviously military men. They were all regular officers, mostly from the SAS, on a course at the School of Infantry.

Why they were in our mess we had no idea. Possibly one of

them had been a national service cadet before joining the regulars and wanted to see if the mess was the same.

They insisted on buying us drinks all evening, although most of their talk was amongst themselves and we listened. It was interesting to hear them talk of past operations. They mentioned "Barney Rubble" quite often. We never worked out who he was.

During the evening one of them became increasingly solicitous and seemed to be very concerned about our spiritual welfare. He introduced himself as Captain Rob Warraker and explained that he was the SAS Padre.

He asked us at what time we had our morning tea break the following morning. We told him that it was from 0950 hours to 1020 hours and he arranged to meet us in the mess at that time for, as he put it, "a little quiet time with the Lord".

We fell into bed at about midnight.

Monday 6 August

After RSM's musters, we moved across to the MT Park for instruction in driving Army trucks. An African soldier, Corporal Enoch, was our instructor.

We spent the first part of the morning in the MT Park area reversing between barrels before breaking for tea and going over to the mess for our meeting with "Padre" Captain Warraker. He didn't appear, and we started to wonder if we had been duped. When we thought about it, he had imbibed more than a few beers the previous evening and on reflection, he had seemed to be a little bit too much the life and soul of the party for a serious man of God.

I met Rob Warraker later, in November 1973, at the SAS Officer's Mess at 2 Brigade in Cranborne. He remembered the evening at Gwelo and was highly amused that we had all pitched up to the mess to meet him and that we had indeed been fooled. He was certainly not a Padre. Sadly Rob Warraker SCR (Silver Cross Rhodesia) was killed in action when shot down while in a Canberra B2 over Malvernia on 12 January 1977. He had been a magnificent soldier.

The rest of the morning found us taking turns to drive the trucks around the private dirt roads in the vicinity of the camp, practising all the things we would need to pass during our driving tests. We knocked off 15 minutes early for lunch.

In the afternoon we went into town with "L" plates and took turns, one of us driving the truck with the rest in the back. At one stage we persuaded Corporal Enoch, much against his better judgment, to stop off at a café for milk shakes.

We were met by Colour Wales when we got back and accused of knocking off 15 minutes early from our morning session without Corporal Enoch's permission. He must have been fed up at our early departure and had reported us.

Again, Colour Wales didn't mince words. "I wasn't as hard on you as I might have been because of the above average age of your course," he said. "I'm beginning to regret that now!"

Our punishment was to plant lawn outside Cadet Wing. We started at 1630 hours and stopped at sundown after giving the area so far planted a good watering.

In the mess afterwards, over a few beers, we tried to see the logic in what had happened. Perhaps, as the senior course, we were perceived to be getting a little too big for our boots, or perhaps they just needed somebody to plant lawn. Who knows? This was the Army, so we didn't spend too much time on the debate and most of us hit the town. We were more than a little fed up.

John Richardson and I linked up with Sel Stevens and had quite a few jars once again. This was becoming a habit.

Tuesday 7 August

The whole morning and part of the afternoon was spent driving around Gwelo again. Later in the afternoon we had a demonstration of the penetrative capabilities of various small arms weapons on the range.

During our defence exercise we had considered ourselves safe behind sandbags in our sangas. Not so, as it turned out. 150 rounds (three belts) were fired from a MAG at 200 yards at a short double wall of sandbags, which demolished it completely. The same was done using an RPD, and although many more rounds were needed the result was the same. A trench or a good shell-scrape was the safest bet in defence.

We finished the active day with another session of lawn planting. After dinner we had a few drinks in the Regular Officer Cadets' Mess at their invitation, a very nice gesture. They commiserated with us on the lawn planting nausea.

Wednesday 8 August

We all arrived at the MT Park for our driving test, to be taken by the MT Sergeant. To our dismay it turned out that the first part of the test was an oral on MT Standing Orders and the Highway Code. We hadn't been told about this.

We proceeded one by one to be tested, in alphabetical order, and one by one our course was failing the oral, which meant one could not proceed to the driving test.

After Pete Addison and Beefy Barlow had come out of the office unsuccessfully, Pete Nupen had the foresight to go and try to locate Corporal Enoch to see if he could get us a copy of either the Standing Orders or the Highway Code. This would enable at least a few of us to read them before being tested. How he did it I don't know, but he got copies of both. However he only got back with them as Digby Neuhoff was going in.

Pete Nupen, John Richardson and I tried our best to read and absorb as much information as we could in the few minutes we had left before our tests. Being last in alphabetical order I had a distinct advantage here. The outcome was that only Pete Nupen and I passed and we were the only ones thus entitled to proceed to the driving test.

While the rest of the course hung around the MT Park, Pete Nupen and I took the driving test. In the end, to my surprise because I didn't think I had driven very well, I was the only one from the course to get a licence to drive a truck. What a waste of time!

Lieutenant McDermott was particularly cross. Apart from anything else, as potential officers, we were supposed to have acquired licences for Land Rovers, not trucks. It had all been, as our course officer put it, "a bloody cock up".

We spent the whole afternoon finishing the lawn planting.

Needless to say we all went on the booze. We began to see why so many people in the Army became dipsomaniacs. We had our final exams next day but this didn't stop us.

Thursday 9 August

We were up early and off to the training area for our tactics practical exam. Each one of was individually examined on our practical map work and voice procedure and then had to prepare and deliver a set of ambush orders. This took all morning.

In the afternoon we had our written tactics exam. Overall, considering our lack of swotting, we all felt that we had done reasonably well.

At the end of the tactics exam we were given the glad tidings that our course was on guard and I was one of the lucky five. This was really annoying, as I had arranged to go for dinner at

John Jones' place at Chaplin School. I had found out about this dinner date from Colour Wales about a week before. Apparently John and Lieutenant Colonel Davidson were chums and John had phoned him and asked him to give me the message about the dinner. Lieutenant Colonel Davidson had relayed the message to Colour Wales to give to me.

Needless to say I had copped a huge "rev" over this and was told in no uncertain terms that the Commandant was "not my bloody answering service". Strangely, Colour Wales didn't seem to mind the fact that I was obviously going to break bounds to attend the dinner. Perhaps he thought Lieutenant Colonel Davidson had given his assent to the arrangement.

After guard mounting I took off anyway, having got myself placed on the 2200-2400 hours and the 0400-0600 hours shifts with Pete Addison very kindly standing in for me in uniform but in our mess.

This was taking a huge chance, as he was supposed to be in the guardhouse at all times and Colour Wales would have known about the dinner if he remembered. I was hoping that he would not connect my dinner date with our late notification of being on guard duty.

We got away with it.

After a pleasant evening with John, his wife Ro, Bill Baker and Steve Ferguson, I took off back to School of Infantry at 2130 hours, got into uniform and made guard duty on time.

Friday 10 August

The first part of the morning was spent writing our Q Accounting and MT Accounting exams. Then Colour Wales took us for a lecture on Combat Tracker Unit. This unit, formed relatively recently, provided trackers, but was primarily concerned with training certain hand-picked soldiers in tracking. This was of particular interest to me as I had met quite a few blokes in this unit while I had been stationed in Kariba with Internal Affairs.

The three I remember well were Andre Rabie, Pete Clemence and "Stretch" Franklin. Tragically, Andre was killed on active service in 1973 by Rhodesian Security Forces while he was operational, in a dreadful mix up.

Colour Wales then left us in the training area near the assault course to practise tracking each other. We did this for a bit but without much success or enthusiasm, and then went to lie in the shade. Colour Wales than came back very surreptitiously and caught us. We spent the next half hour doubling up and down the nearby kopje.

We waited all afternoon in our lecture room for a lecture from Lieutenant McDermott on border control. He never pitched up, so at about 1630 hours most of us headed off on leave to Salisbury. I took my Mazda bakkie with Pete Addison and Digby Neuhoff for company. I dropped them off at the Jameson Hotel and drove out to Borrowdale to stay the weekend with Mervyn Thompson.

For the first time ever there was no worry about studying for exams. With two weeks to go to the end of the course, essentially only our coin exercise remained. This was to be held in the Matopos Tribal Trust Land with our intake from Llewellin.

Mervyn and I drove across to the Kamfinsa Hotel for a few beers. It was the end of the second school term and Mervyn was in celebration mode.

Mervyn was an irrepressible and irreverent Northern Ireland protestant, and on a night out with him, or on any occasion, anything could happen. Once when he was umpiring a cricket team at St George's College on one of the lower fields, he and his opposite number, Father Nixon, were walking up to the pavilion on the main field for the tea break between innings.

They walked past a vegetable garden that had recently been treated with manure. "To be sure" said Mervyn, noticing the aroma, "it smells as though they've buried a nun."

As it turned out it was a quiet evening. We hadn't bumped into any republican Irishmen.

Saturday 11 August

I went into Salisbury for the morning and bought a few things, then went to have lunch and spend the afternoon with my folks. The evening was spent having a night on the town.

We first hit the George Hotel for a couple of beers before deciding where to eat. I asked Mervyn if he ate Chinese. He said he had never actually eaten them, so couldn't comment. We ate at the Golden Dragon, but stuck to sweet and sour pork.

We finished the evening at Le Coq d'Or.

Sunday 12 August

After two late nights, I had a quiet day and apart from a quick trip up the road to the Helensvale shopping centre for re-supplies, mostly booze, I relaxed around the house. Mid-afternoon I picked up Pete and Digby from the Jameson Hotel. On the way to Gwelo Digby collected his car, which had needed a bit of work done on the engine, at Hunter's Road. The bloke who had been working on Digby's car was an amazing Afrikaans baas, a sort of latter day Sarel Cilliers.

Finally I got an early night.

Monday 13 August

The day started with a lecture on land mines and terrorist tactics. The land mines used by terrs were anti-vehicle with 15 lbs of HE, and quite capable of blowing a vehicle or part of a vehicle to a height of 15 feet in addition to doing tremendous damage due to fragmentation. So far they had only been planted on dirt roads, but they seemed to be planted indiscriminately. Many civilian vehicles, including bakkies, buses and trucks, were blown up, resulting in horrible casualties.

The only technique at our disposal for detecting land mines on dirt roads was to look ahead for obviously disturbed ground.

Terrs were at pains to avoid contact with security forces, although they were quite happy to hit perceived soft targets such as farmhouses. They were primarily engaged in winning over the rural population to their cause, often employing the most intimidating tactics. Horrendous reprisals would be enacted on anyone suspected of collaboration with security forces.

They would arrive in the night in an African village and hold pungwes, meetings which would last all night. During these they would extol their virtues while denigrating the security forces and assure them of a wonderful future in which they would inherit all the white man's possessions and live in a land of milk and honey.

Of late the terrs, when initiating an ambush on security forces (not a frequent occurrence) or an attack on a farmhouse, would do so just before the sun went down or early in the evening. This would mean any follow-up would be delayed until daylight, allowing many hours for their escape. Often they would encourage mujibas (boy supporters of their cause) to drive cattle over their tracks to confuse the trackers.

Their tactic if involved in a contact with security forces was to "bombshell". This meant to run in different directions, to make a follow up on the whole group impossible and eventually, usually after dark, to RV at predesignated land marks. As they moved through the bush they would constantly change the RV to prominent or well-known features closer to their position as the previous one receded into the distance.

We spent the last part of the morning preparing for our final coin exercise, getting our kit together.

After lunch we were given our appointments. I was made "Second Lieutenant" with Digby Neuhoff as my platoon "Sergeant". We drew weapons and set off for Llewellin Barracks. We arrived, for the first time since leaving in April, at about 1530hrs.

We three "Second Lieutenants", Sanderson, Addison and Lenegan, had to sign for most of the stores necessary for the exercise, quite a palaver. I took over the stores for my platoon, No. 6 Platoon, from Colour Sergeant Botha and had to sign for everything.

There was an awful lot of equipment to take responsibility for including ration packs, picks and shovels, maps, compasses and, of all things, a water bowser which had to be filled the next day. Having signed for it all, the storeroom and surrounding fence were securely locked and the keys given to me.

We were given a very short briefing by Lieutenant McDermott, who told us roughly where in the Matopos tribal trust lands we would be going and letting us know that each platoon would have seconded to us an African messenger from Internal Affairs who was familiar with the area and that it would be advisable to use him during the exercise. As usual, demonstration troops would be the "enemy".

Trucks, with drivers, for transporting the troops would be provided by 11 Supply and Transport Platoon (11 ST).

We then moved across to a small barrack room next to the Officers' Mess to spend the night. We were allowed in the mess itself, but only in the ladies' room, which had its own bar with a barman and a large dining table. For the first night of the exercise at least we were in the lap of luxury. No ladies, unfortunately.

Tuesday 14 August

After breakfast we moved across to the lecture rooms to meet our platoons to give them a short briefing, as much as we knew, issue them with equipment and then give orders for loading and order of march.

It was discovered that the bowser that had been issued to me was unserviceable, something to do with the bearings, and another had to be brought at short notice. By this time we had to leave and I was unable to get it filled.

We set off for the Matopos TTL, debussed and took up a position of all-round defence in an area of ground next to the Matopos Police Station. "Platoon Commanders" then went to the Police Station for orders from Lieutenant McDermott, who was taking the role of "Company Commander". They were pretty perfunctory. There were terrorists in the area. Nos. 4, 5 and 6 platoons were allocated certain areas in which to operate with boundary northings and eastings being given, together with a grid reference for an initial overnight rough base camp. That was about it. Using this information, we "Platoon Commanders" had to return to our platoons and prepare and give orders.

I drew Lieutenant McDermott to listen to my orders, while the others gave their orders in front of other DS. I knew enough by now to spin these out, leaving no stone unturned, and thought I had done a good job. Lieutenant McDermott was not of this opinion however, and I copped what seemed by now to be the almost inevitable "rev". "Sanderson, your orders were not nearly detailed enough. You're "cuffing it". Jack yourself up."

Our platoon now left the other two and set off for our rough base position, getting there in the late afternoon. I set it up, siting positions and got them started digging shell-scrapes. I sent a "Corporal" with a section to do a 360, then, with everything in place, got another section together to go on a recce to try to find a final base position with if possible an alternative.

This proved to be more difficult than I had anticipated. It was impossible in the area we were in to get away from habitable areas. There was no water readily available, and worst of all I was unable to get communications with Company HQ. We walked from place to place. One or two reasonable positions had to be passed up, as I could get no comms at all.

Eventually, at about 2200hrs, from what I thought could be a reasonable base position, I got through to Company HQ and a very tired-sounding voice responded. I couldn't help thinking that the radio operator had been sleeping and had not heard me trying to get through all this time. Nevertheless, we now had comms, so I decided that this would be our final base position.

Throughout the war people had difficulty with comms. I remember some years into the war, an American who was an officer in the RLI giving us a talk on the Vietnam War, comparing and contrasting it with the war in Rhodesia. With regard to radio communication he articulated his considered opinion.

"In Rhodesia your comms are shit. You have the same equipment that we had in Vietnam, so it should work, but it doesn't. I don't know if it is the minerals in the hills or what, but your comms are shit."

I still hadn't found an alternative position and my section, although they hadn't complained, were pretty exhausted. I sent them back to the rough base and continued to look for the alternative position on my own. After all, I reasoned, this whole thing was an exercise, not the real thing, and I could move more quickly on my own.

I found a position, not very good for all round defence, but passable and with good comms.

Wednesday 15 August

I got back to the rough base position at 0200hrs. After a scrambled breakfast we drove to my selected final base position.

I had just indicated a 12 to 6 o'clock line and relative to this allocated positions for a vehicle park, initial shell-scrapes to each section, drivers and the African messenger. I was about to send out a 360 patrol when Lieutenant McDermott came up to me and told me that he couldn't get comms with the company HQ.

Like an idiot, I had started to prepare the position before checking comms, a fundamental error. The fact that I had got comms the night before was irrelevant. I now had the embarrassment of calling my section commanders in and telling them not to dig – some had started already – and to hold their positions while I jumped into a Land Rover with Lieutenant McDermott to locate another base camp.

I told him that I had done a recce during the night and had found an alternative site. He told me to take us to it. I guided him in with my heart in my mouth, hoping that we would get comms when we got there. I was lucky, because when we got there comms were fives. We drove back to the platoon.

On the way he asked me what time I got in from my recce. I told him 0200 hrs. He then asked me if I had done the recce on my own. I suppose I had been using the first person singular all the time. I had to admit that, although I had taken a section out for the first part of the recce, I had done the recce of the alternative position on my own. Needless to say I got a blast for this and an admonishment for being too soft on my men by letting them off early. I made a mental note never to go "untac" again on an exercise.

He did grudgingly admit, however, that it had been a good idea of mine to do a recce during the night and as I was getting out of the Land Rover he smiled, the first time I had ever seen him do this, and said "Carry on Lieutenant." I didn't know if he was being sarcastic or suggesting that I might be in line to get a commission.

We moved to the alternative position. The DS established a camp a few hundred yards away and we settled down into daily routine.

I sent Digby Neuhoff with one section and two other sections, with "Corporals" from Llewellin in charge, on day-long patrols. It was also necessary for me to fill our water bowser, as most men had finished the water in their two water-bottles.

I consulted the Internal Affairs messenger and it turned out that there was an Intaf hut with a borehole water supply from a tap about three miles from our position. He told us that unfortunately there was no hose available for the tap so we had to take a bucket with us and fill the bowser using this. A section of us took turns to do this. It occupied some time.

I arrived back at our base just as the day patrols were coming in with nothing to report. I had thought that with the "enemy" out there they might have had a "contact", or at least have spotted some "tracks".

It was good to eventually get some sleep with only the inevitable guard duty for each section, two hours on six hours off, to interrupt it.

Thursday 16 August

We had another day of routine. I sent two more patrols out, the route based on "info about terr movement" given to us by Lieutenant McDermott. Colour Wales came and spent some time telling me what was wrong with my base position. It was pretty much what I had thought when I first sited it. His greatest criticism was on the grounds that I had not avoided populated areas. Testament to this was the fact that large numbers of African children from a kraal about a mile away had surrounded the camp to see what was happening and were peeping through the trees at us.

I still maintain that it would have been impossible to have sited a base within our designated area far enough away from kraals to prevent these visits. I kept my mouth shut though and took the "rev".

I spent some time during the day going around to the section positions giving orders for their improvement, such as requiring deeper shell-scrapes and better bivvies. I was impressed at the way the troops complied. Obviously training at Llewellin had paid off.

The patrols came back once again with nothing to report and we settled down for the night.

Friday 17 August

Early in the morning our appointments were changed. I was now "Platoon Sergeant". Digby was made "Platoon Commander". He immediately sent me off on a long patrol with two sections, but after about half an hour we got a radio message to return to base.

When we got back, preparations for a "follow up" were underway. Another patrol had come across "terrorist tracks". The platoon then proceeded on foot with a tracker section in the lead, having loaded all superfluous equipment in the trucks, which departed for the Company HQ position.

It was a hot day and by 1700hrs most of us were down to one full water bottle. We had started with two. We filled up at a dam using our water purification tablets. We camped the night on a cold hill in a position of all-round defence.

Saturday 18 August

Appointment changes were made again. Digby remained as "Platoon Commander" but I was now a "Corporal". It was always easier to have an NCO appointment, with far fewer things to worry about. For the first time I wondered if it might not be too bad a thing to leave School of Infantry with a non-commissioned rank. Life during the last seven months of National Service might be a lot simpler.

Throughout the morning we had bad guti and all of us were experiencing a sense of humour failure. Ponchos are not entirely water proof and we were getting more than a little irritated.

We followed up all day with no incident, carrying our rifles at the port at all times. Throughout our training we had moved in this way. Slings, although issued, were never used.

A couple of blokes in my section tried to light up cigarettes for a quick smoke while on the march. I was pretty fed up in general and almost found delight in giving them a "rev" and telling them to wait until we had a break and took up a position of all-round defence. They grumbled a bit but discipline asserted itself, even though I had no official rank, and we moved on.

We camped on a dwala (a huge outcrop of rock, sometimes the size of a large hill). The rocky terrain made it difficult to erect bivvies and I got my section to set them up using rocks to hold them down. Some sections didn't bother to put them up – not my problem, I was just a "Corporal". During the night the heavy guti returned and they paid the price.

Sunday 19 August

By dawn the weather was clear. We continued the follow up all morning, on the way being guided, by the Intaf messenger, to a water pool deep inside a rocky outcrop where we could fill our water bottles. His local knowledge was invaluable, as we certainly would not have found this supply on our own.

The trackers had picked up "fresh spoor" and we stepped up the pace with no breaks for several hours. We stopped for a quick lunch gleaned from the ration packs, then moved on.

At about 1500hrs we had a "contact" initiated by a "terr" ambush. We went through the usual EA drills and finished with several "kills" and a few "prisoners".

In the early evening we were taken back to an area near the Company HQ by Land Rover and F250s, small one-ton trucks. Digby sited positions in a new base camp but gave no instructions to dig shell-scrapes.

I queried this but Digby, like me, had had enough of this "playing soldiers" and had decided that we would not dig them and let the men rest. Once again in a real situation we would of course have dug shell-scrapes, but I suppose he thought "To hell with it!"

Monday 20 August

Lieutenant Mc Dermott and some other DS arrived bright and early as we were putting breakfast together and gave us the new appointments. I was once again "Platoon Commander" with Digby as my "Sergeant". I was fully expecting that he would comment on the fact that we hadn't dug shell-scrapes, but to my surprise he said nothing. It wasn't like him to miss an opportunity for a "rev".

We got on with base routine. Later in the morning

Lieutenant Colonel Thompson, CO DRR, and Major Morris, B Company Commander, came round and asked disapprovingly why we hadn't dug shell-scrapes. Would I ever learn? So much for my resolve of a few days earlier, I had "gone untac".

I called in my section commanders and got them to start the troops digging. Putting myself back into "tac" mode I went across to the Company HQ to update myself on the "situation" and to get an exact fix on our current position. We had known our position up until the "contact" the previous day, but had not traced the route we had followed when being taken out by the vehicles.

It was just as well that I did this, as in the late afternoon we got the orders to move to another base position a few miles away and I was able to get there.

We started to dig in at the new position when the glad tidings were announced that the exercise was over. We were told that we could now go "untac", with the proviso that guard would still have to be posted.

It was bliss not to have to think about much and to stop the role play. As I said before, I never got the hang of it. I wondered how the other members of our course had done on the exercise. Apart from Digby, I hadn't seen anyone from our course for days.

Rob Mutch was a mile up the road as "Platoon Commander" of his platoon and using his initiative, as he usually did, had managed to buy quite a few chickens from the locals for a sumptuous supper. His troops fared better than mine that night.

Tuesday 21 August

The whole company rendezvoused and we took off for Llewellin. Equipment was handed in, miraculously with no loss, and our course set off for Gwelo. We arrived just after lunch, handed in weapons and were given the afternoon off.

It was great to have a leisurely hot shower and get eight days dirt off us. We then hit Gwelo en masse and had more than a few ales in various pubs before supper at the mess and a relatively early bed.

Wednesday 22 August

We drew weapons, live ammunition and grenades. This would be the last time at Gwelo that we would have anything to do with the armoury. We climbed aboard an RL and headed towards Selukwe for a jungle lane exercise. Hayden Whisken was on the exercise with us once again as a medic.

This was a little bit like our shotgun exercise when we did our battle camp a few weeks earlier. We would take turns to walk down a path through thick bush with our FNs and fire at semi-concealed human figure targets on either side. At the end of the path we would have to pull the pin on an M67 grenade, throw it at three dummies "sitting around a fire", count three seconds and get down.

Each "jungle lane" would take some time to set up and the

number of hits on the targets would have to be counted at the end of each walk. It was probably the most relaxed bit of training we had had so far. There was no shouting, "revving" or anything other than constructive criticism.

We fired off any remaining ammunition at targets set up at the base of a hill. On the way back I was with Colour Wales in the front of the RL and found out a little bit more about him. I found out that he was an Ellis Robins old boy. I asked him how he would cope with the fact that some of us would be commissioned and that he would have to salute us, when he was an infinitely better soldier than any of us.

He replied that this was the Army and that initially one always saluted the rank. This had nothing to do with the individual receiving the salute. It was all part of preserving the structure and the discipline. I thought this was a brilliant answer.

When we got back to Gwelo he said "You have a licence, haven't you?" He then handed the keys of the motor park to me and told me to park the truck and bring the keys of the motor park and the RL to him in the Sergeants' and Warrant Officers' Mess, where he intended to sink a few beers. We cleaned and handed in our weapons for the last time.

We spent a convivial evening in the mess. It was a little bit of a "last supper" as we were due to get our official appointments the next morning. We had all worked hard on the course, and having come this far most of us wanted that commission.

Thursday 23 August

We met at Taungup for the last time for a talk from Lieutenant McDermott on what was expected of an officer. He began by telling us that we would at least have the rank of Corporal. If we were commissioned, we were told, it was not to go to our heads. We were still hugely inexperienced in the military and although we would be receiving salutes from NCOs, including Warrant Officers, and would be called "sir", they didn't mean it.

We were to salute very smartly back and show the utmost respect at all times, replying to their compliment by using their rank, Corporal, Sergeant, Colour, Staff and, for WO2s, Sergeant Major. Under no circumstances were we to refer to WO1s as Sergeant Major. This would be a complete insult. RSM Collyer, for example, would be referred to as either RSM or Mr Collyer.

As Second Lieutenants we would call any officer senior to us "sir" at all times until we were told otherwise by them. We would always refer to them as "sir" in front of the troops and always call Majors and higher ranks "sir".

We were to steer clear of soldiers when they were drunk and disorderly and not try to discipline them under these circumstances. We were to leave it to the NCOs, as any assault on us would lead to a far more severe penalty being meted out to the soldier than if we stayed out of the way.

Having digested all this, we were told to wait a little way up the hill above Taungup to be called down to one of the huts near Cadet Wing to have our final interviews and get our appointments. It was the moment of truth.

We waited, out of sight of the hut, until a Corporal from the Pay Corps came to fetch us and take us to the hut one by one in alphabetical order. I would be the last to go in.

All sorts of things were going through our minds as we waited with very little chatter going on between us. Rob Mutch slightly eased the tension. "At least they have to make us Corporals," he said.

Our numbers gradually diminished as each was called away. There was no way of telling what appointments were being made. Each interview was taking about ten minutes.

Finally, I was on my own on the hill. While I waited I tried to think logically about my chances of getting commissioned. Had I made too many mistakes? Was I perceived as too "soft with my men"? And was I insufficiently military? How would my father take it if I came out a Corporal? He had been commissioned during the Second World War.

I was finally called to the hut. I entered, saluted Lieutenant McDermott and was told to sit down. Colour Wales was seated next to him.

Lieutenant McDermott asked me how I thought I had done. I said that I had done my very best but battled at times to role play and that I had made quite a few mistakes during my training. He replied that I hadn't made more than anyone else, less than most. This seemed promising.

He asked me if I liked telling people what to do. Here we go, I thought, but answered that I was quite happy to tell people what to do if it was necessary. Lieutenant McDermott gave a little chuckle and said that it was always necessary. Colour Wales was grinning.

There seemed to be something in his manner that made me fear the worst and I had an awful feeling that I had "blown it", so much so that his next words surprised me.

"We're commissioning you, Sanderson" said Lieutenant McDermott, "and you will be with 11 ST Platoon, Rhodesian Army Service Corps, Llewellin Barracks."

I was relieved to be commissioned, but disappointed that I would not be with the independent company. This must have shown on my face because Lieutenant McDermott said that I seemed to be disappointed. I replied that I had hoped to be with 131 but was essentially in the Army to do what they wanted me to do. I was told that I was now a member of an exclusive group and that the highest standards of conduct were expected of me.

I left and was directed by the Corporal to another hut next door and told to go in. When I entered there were four others inside, Pete Addison, Charlie Lenegan, Rob Mutch and Digby Neuhoff. There was much handshaking and back patting, unfortunately tempered by the fact that three of our course were not there.

Pete, Rob and Digby had been posted to 3 Independent Company and Charlie had got Artillery. Beefy Barlow was a

Sergeant and John Richardson and Pete Nupen were Corporals, all posted to 3 Independent Company.

We went across to the QM store to get our epaulettes and chevrons with Colour Wales. They only had four sets of Second Lieutenant's pips, issued in alphabetical order, so I missed out. I would have to get my epaulettes when I joined my unit. Nobody was to wear their rank until they joined their units next Wednesday after a short leave.

Fortunately, when I got to the Llewellin Barracks Officers' Mess a few days later, another officer staying there, Captain Roger Pettit, had a set of Second Lieutenant's pips and gave them to me. Roger had served in the Australian Army in Vietnam before joining the Rhodesian Army. His brother, WO2 John Pettit, had been killed in action 4 April 1970 near Dak Seang while operating with the Americans and the Montagnards. He was posthumously awarded the American Silver Star for personal heroism, professional competence and devotion to duty.

The afternoon was spent handing in kit and obtaining clearance from all the requisite departments and important people at School of Infantry. My parents were coming down for the passing-out ceremony and the evening dance due to take place next day. They had booked in at the Midlands Hotel.

After clearance I went around to the hotel to see if they had arrived. They had, and I gave them the news about my commission. I was worried that my father might be disappointed that I was not going with the infantry where he had been, but this did not seem to bother him at all.

I left them and went back to School of Infantry to have a few celebratory drinks. Only John seemed to be really disappointed with his appointment. I was disappointed too, as I really felt that he should have been commissioned. He seemed very practical and, on the academic side, in his final exams he had tied for second place; ours not to reason why.

John and I hit the Midlands Hotel for the last time for a meal. I did my very best to cheer him up, but he was understandably very unhappy.

Friday 24 August

At 0815hrs we had the course photograph with Lieutenant McDermott and Colour Wales in greens and us in stick kit on the edge of the parade ground. None of us ever got a copy of this photograph. Copies were supposed to be forwarded by post to us at our units. What happened to them no one knows. Digby Neuhoff tried to get a copy, dropping into School of Infantry several times in 1973 and 1974, but with no success.

In late March 1980, after the war, I was on an exercise with artillery and other units (I had transferred over to Rhodesian Artillery in 1975). I was staying at the School of Infantry Officers' Mess the night before the exercise began. I walked across to the National Service Officer Cadet Mess to see if a copy of the photograph that we hadn't received was up on the wall with all the other courses at Gwelo over the years. They had been moved there from Moyale. The photo of Intake 130 was there, the photo of Intake 132 was there and so were all the others, but nothing for Intake 131.

After the photo we changed into weapon training order and waited to greet our relatives at the mess. The presentation of the Commandants Award for the best cadet and the final address from Lieutenant Colonel Davidson took place in the mess area.

We had to introduce our relatives to our course officer and instructor, the Commandant, Major Pelham and CSM Hallamore.

I was a little surprised that Lieutenant Colonel Davidson, when introduced to my father, called him "sir". I shouldn't have been really. We were of such an age that most of our fathers would have served in the Second World War and Lieutenant Colonel Davidson would have naturally respected this service. My father had been a Major in the British Army in 1943, thirty years earlier.

As best cadet, Pete Addison was presented with a School of Infantry plaque. He had done well and the award was thoroughly deserved.

At 1030hrs we had morning tea, followed by a short demonstration in the training area run by the course. We organized for all the fathers to fire the FN, demonstrated the firing of the MAG, ran the assault course, simulated GAC using smoke and fired coloured and Icarus flares.

At 1200hrs there was a sherry party, after which we had time off until the passing-out dance at 1930hrs. We spent the afternoon decorating the mess for this.

At 1900hrs I went to pick up my date for the evening. I didn't know any girls in Gwelo, so I had asked one of the secretaries at the School of Infantry to the dance. She had very graciously accepted.

Everyone was relaxed and we all danced until about midnight. It was a good evening but sad also, especially for me. We had been through a lot together and I was going my separate way. I took my date home and went back to School of Infantry to spend the last night.

Saturday 26 August 1973

In the morning we tidied up the mess, returned a camouflage net we had used with the décor to the stores and then took off in various directions for our short leave before reporting to our units.

And so it all ended.

I often wonder what happened with many of those blokes on the course. I bumped into a few of them over the years and I have an idea where some of them are now, but am only currently in touch with Digby Neuhoff, teaching at Woodbridge School in England and Pete Addison and Charlie Lenegan both in Perth, Australia. It would be good to touch base again with the others.

Index